Expressions

WORKBOOK

GEOFFREY BROUGHTON

OVERSEAS STUDENT
UNIT
CHICHESTER COLLEGE
OF TECHNOLOGY
WESTGATE FIELDS
CHICHESTER
PO19 1SB

COLLINS ELT · LONDON AND GLASGOW

Collins ELT
8 Grafton Street
London W1X 3LA

© Geoffrey Broughton 1987

10 9 8 7 6 5 4 3 2 1

First published 1987

All rights reserved. No part of this book may be reproduced, stored in a retrieval system, or transmitted in any form or by any means, electronic, mechanical, photocopying, recording or otherwise, without the prior permission in writing of the Publisher.

Printed in Great Britain by Butler & Tanner Ltd, Frome and London

ISBN 0 00 370642 7

Design by Gina Smart
Illustrations by Gina Smart and Mike Strudwick
Cover design by Gina Smart

Acknowledgements

The author and publishers are grateful to the following for permission to reproduce copyright material (page numbers in brackets):

The Department of Transport (7); British Airways (8); Picturepoint, London for *Mona Lisa* by Leonardo da Vinci (12); Graphische Sammlung Albertina, Vienna for *Maximilian I* by Albrecht Dürer (1518) (12); the Trustees of the Imperial War Museum, London (13); George Philip & Son Ltd for text and pie charts from *Philips New World Atlas* (20); Albright–Knox Art Gallery, Buffalo, New York for *Dynamism of a Dog on a Leash* by Giacomo Balla (1912, $35\frac{3}{8} \times 43\frac{1}{4}$, oil on canvas), Bequest of A. Conger Goodyear and gift of George F. Goodyear, 1964 (44); ADAGP, Paris and COSMOPRESS, Geneva © 1986, and the Tate Gallery, London for *Comedy* by Paul Klee (44); Spectrum Colour Library (cover photo).

CONTENTS

- Exercises — 1
- Crosswords — 52
- Some English idioms — 61
- Echo phrases — 65
- Irreversible phrases — 65
- Some English similes — 66
- Functions — 67
- Lexicon — 75

Unit 1

INSTANT DIALOGUE

He *I wonder why Colin (1) last night.*
She *Well it's hardly the first time he's (1) is it?*
He *But why did he (1) with Pat all of a sudden?*
She *Don't you know? Pat has been (2) about Mary.*
He *Then perhaps Colin has good reason.*

References
(1) C6, L1.3.12
(2) L1.3.18

CUED DIALOGUE

References: B1, C5, C7, C13, C15, C21, L1.4.12

Situation Charles was gloomy last night. Possible reasons are his recent exam results, his non-smoking campaign and his damaged motorcycle. Ann knows the true reason: Trudy has told Charles their friendship is over.

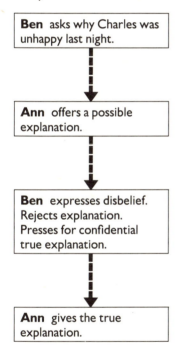

Ben asks why Charles was unhappy last night.	Direct	*Why...?* *Do you know why...?*
	Indirect	*I wonder why...* *I can't think why...*
Ann offers a possible explanation.	As statement	*Perhaps it was because of...* *I reckon he's upset about...*
	As question	*Do you think it's his...?* *Could it be he's sad about...?*
Ben expresses disbelief. Rejects explanation. Presses for confidential true explanation.		*I can't think...* *No, it's something more serious...*
	Direct	*Come on, you can tell me...* *Between you and me, what's...*
	Indirect	*I can keep a secret you know...* *I believe if you wanted to, you could...*
Ann gives the true explanation.	Direct	*Well, it's Trudy. She's finished with him.* *Trudy told him it's finished.*
	Indirect	*Perhaps you'd be miserable if your girl-friend...* *How would you feel if...*

THOUGHTS, HOT AND COLD

unemotional	emotional	
		insult
		anticipation
		persuasion
		enjoyment
		hostility
		reference
		anxiety
		bullying
		satisfaction
		opposition

ANGER NOUNS

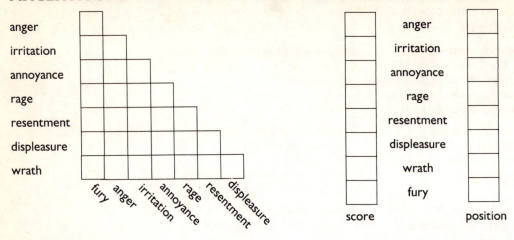

FILL IN THE BLANKS

Verb	Noun	Adjective
		pitiful
protect		
	compassion	
	friendship	
		sympathetic
tolerate		
	benevolence	
consider		
	mercy	
console		

EMOTIONAL QUIZ

	true		false	
Losing one's temper is a form of self-indulgence.				
It is foolish to grieve when an old person dies.				
No person alive has ever been completely terrified.				
People only vote for politicians they admire.				
All ambition is a form of greed.				
We do not owe our parents any gratitude.				
Fear of death lies behind all religion.				
The one purpose of art is to please.				
No animals are repulsive.				
To feel contempt for someone is always a weakness.				

total........... total...........

TEST YOURSELF ● Listen to the passage being read to you. Then read the questions below. Listen to the passage again before writing your answers in the boxes.

1. *Johnson was furious because—*
   a it was his birthday
   b his toast was cold
   c the postman had forgotten him
   d there were no birthday cards

2. *Showering and dressing, he was looking forward to seeing—*
   a a pile of envelopes for him
   b his toast and marmalade
   c Joan
   d the doormat

3. *Johnson was most disappointed that—*
   a his friends had forgotten him
   b his elation left him
   c Joan had forgotten his birthday
   d his toast was getting cold

4. *He became cheerful again when he thought he would find .... on the breakfast table.*
   a toast and marmalade
   b birthday greetings
   c a lot of envelopes
   d Joan's card

5. *When he sat down to breakfast he felt—*
   a ashamed
   b angry
   c delighted
   d jealous

6. *Reading Joan's card he began to feel—*
   a ashamed
   b delighted
   c furious
   d idiotic

7. *Johnson had forgotten that—*
   a it was his birthday
   b it was Sunday
   c there was no post on Sundays
   d the postman came on Saturday

8. *Which is not true?*
   a Joan was holding his cards
   b Joan had hidden his cards
   c The cards were under his plate
   d His cards had arrived on Saturday

9. *Joan told him a lot of people .... him.*
   a adored
   b abhorred
   c admired
   d doted on

10. *Johnson felt .... both at the same time.*
    a guilty and glad
    b happy and angry
    c angry and delighted
    d ashamed and delighted

Unit 2

PERSONAL CHECKLIST

1 Documents	2 Clothes	3 Accessories	4 Personal	5 Equipment
☐	☐	☐	☐	☐
☐	☐	☐	☐	☐
☐	☐	☐	☐	☐
☐	☐	☐	☐	☐
☐	☐	☐	☐	☐
☐	☐	☐	☐	☐
☐	☐	☐	☐	☐
☐	☐	☐	☐	☐
☐	☐	☐	☐	☐

DAMAGE VERBS ● Write the twenty verbs in the correct squares.

break   injure
bruise   kill
buckle   lame
cripple   ruin
crush   rust
damage   scratch
dent   twist
destroy   warp
explode   wound
fracture   wreck

person/parts of person

machine/parts of machine

WHAT GOES WITH WHAT? ● Which verbs go with which substances?
Ask: 'Can we break glass/cloth?' etc. Put a tick in the appropriate boxes.

	bone	muscle	stone	glass	plastic	metal	paper	cloth
break								
fracture								
strain								
tear								
scratch								
chip								
grind								
melt								
crease								

● Now do the exercise again in your own language. Compare the two sets of results.

BRAXTON CAR RENTAL   Damage Declaration

112–114 London Road   Norton

Vehicle.................. Registration number.................. Date out..................
Hirer: Name:................. Address.. Tel:............

Mark position of damage below   Details of damage:

Instruments:

Controls:

Upholstery:

Declaration by hirer: I agree that all damage or wear to the vehicle at the time of rental has been recorded above, and that I accept full responsibility for any further damage or wear to the vehicle at the end of the period of rental.

Signature..................... Date................. Vehicle Checker..........................

ST. MARTIN'S HOSPITAL

From: Deputy Administrator   To: Reception
Subject: Coach crash: Information for Date: 17th May
          phone enquiries

Ward C	Alan Burgess	Broken ribs, Perforated lungs	Poorly
	William Duke	Minor cuts and bruises	Comfortable
	John Harlow	Crushed foot, fractured leg	Stable
	Geoffrey Mossop	Ruptured spleen, other internal injuries	V. poorly
	Colin Rhodes	Head injuries	Seriously ill
Ward E	Amy Field	Cuts to head and face, fractured wrist	Comfortable
	Mahinder Kaur	Lacerations to face and chest	Stable
	Shelley Luff	Left leg amputated	Stable
	Linda Slack	Superficial cuts and bruises only	Comfortable
	Mary Stoney	Concussion, some damage to spine	Poorly

CUED DIALOGUES

Situation   Friend/relative telephoning hospital reception.

> **A** introduces self: asks after named victim.
> **B** gently reports patient's condition.
> **A** reacts and asks for details of injuries.
> **B** gently reports injuries.
> **A** thanks B and rings off.
> **B** says goodbye.

References: A3, A11, B1, C8

TEST YOURSELF ● Listen to the passage being read to you. Then read the questions below. Listen to the passage again before writing your answers in the boxes.

1. *The scene took place in—*
   a Simon's house
   b Blackstone's house
   c the Hilton bar
   d a hotel lounge

2. *Besides Simon there were .... other named people present.*
   a two
   b three
   c four
   d five

3. *When Simon first knew Stephanie, she was a—*
   a red-head
   b blonde
   c film star
   d stage actress

4. *Simon was waiting for Stephanie with—*
   a Lucy
   b Blackstone
   c another man
   d Hilton

5. *When Stephenie entered, Simon—*
   a stood up
   b sat down
   c waved to her
   d took her arm

6. *Stephanie's skin was the colour of—*
   a a cherry
   b an apricot
   c a peach
   d a berry

7. *Simon remembered she had a blemish on her—*
   a left cheek
   b right cheek
   c right forehead
   d left forehead

8. *Her nose appeared ....: than before.*
   a paler
   b neater
   c smaller
   d straighter

9. *She reminded Simon of an advertisement because of her—*
   a hair
   b teeth
   c toothpaste
   d smile

10. *Blackstone only permitted Simon to .... Stephanie.*
    a shake hands with
    b smile at
    c put his arms round
    d talk to

Unit 3

CUED DIALOGUES

References: A2, A3, A6, A8, A11, B1

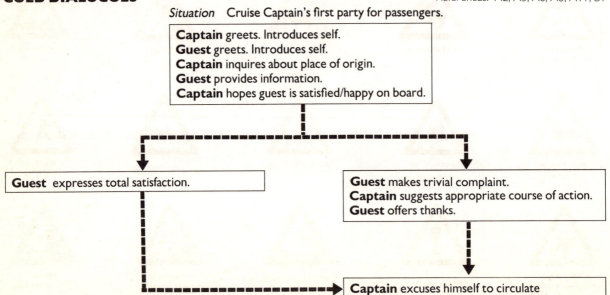

Situation   Cruise Captain's first party for passengers.

Captain greets. Introduces self.
Guest greets. Introduces self.
Captain inquires about place of origin.
Guest provides information.
Captain hopes guest is satisfied/happy on board.

Guest expresses total satisfaction.

Guest makes trivial complaint.
Captain suggests appropriate course of action.
Guest offers thanks.

Captain excuses himself to circulate

Situation Air hostess making first contact with passengers.

Hostess inquires if all is well.
Passenger thanks her and is content.
Hostess asks if passenger has been to that destination before.

Passenger tells her never.
Hostess comments favourably on it.
Passenger expresses pleasurable anticipation.

Passenger tells her frequently.
Hostess inquires passenger's opinion of country.
Passenger comments favourably on it.

Hostess expresses best wishes for remainder of flight and stay.

TRAFFIC SIGNS

 No motor vehicles

 No vehicles with over 12 seats

 National speed limit applies

 No cycling

 No right turn

 No entry

 No vehicles including load over weight shown (in tonnes)

 No goods vehicles over maximum gross weight shown (in tonnes)

 No overtaking

 Give priority to vehicles from opposite direction

 Maximum speed

 No U turns

 Height limit (e.g. low bridge)

 Wild animals

 Cattle

 Road works

 Uneven road

 Wild horses or ponies

 Slippery road

 Worded warning sign

 Overhead electric cable

 Pedestrian crossing

 Low-flying aircraft or sudden aircraft noise

 Other danger

 Opening or swing bridge

 Quayside or river bank

 Falling or fallen rocks

Dangerous articles in baggage

For safety reasons, dangerous articles such as those listed below, must not be carried in passengers' baggage.

Compressed gases – (Deeply refrigerated, flammable, non-flammable and poisonous) such as butane, oxygen, liquid nitrogen, aqualung cylinders

Compressed gas cylinders   Aqualungs

Corrosives such as acids, alkalis, mercury and wet cell batteries

Wet cell batteries   Apparatus containing mercury

Explosives, munitions, fireworks and flares

Hand guns   Ammunition including blank cartridges   Fireworks

Pistol caps

Flammable liquids and solids such as lighter fuel, matches, paints, thinners, fire-lighters

 Lighters that need inverting before ignition   Lighter fuel
 Lighter refills
Matches may be carried on the person

Radioactive materials

Brief-cases and attaché cases with installed alarm devices

Oxidising materials such as bleaching powder, peroxides

Poisons and infectious substances such as insecticides, weed-killers and live virus materials

Other dangerous articles such as magnetised material, offensive or irritating materials

Medicines and toiletries in limited quantities which are necessary or appropriate for the passenger during the journey, such as hairsprays, perfumes and medicines containing alcohol may be carried. Many of these listed articles can be carried as air cargo provided they are packed in accordance with cargo regulations.

Further information is available on request.

LIKELIHOOD

● Arrange the following in four columns according to the strength of likelihood expressed.

There's no chance.	It's not impossible.	It's uncertain.	It could well be.
Little possibility.	Possibly.	It's on the cards.	It hasn't a cat in hell's chance.
A slight possibility.	It's out of the question.	It's rather improbable.	It's almost bound to be.
It's quite likely.	Probably.	Not the remotest chance.	It might just be.
There's a good chance.	Perhaps.	The odds are in favour.	Not the slightest chance.

Strong likelihood	**Some likelihood**	**Little likelihood**	**No likelihood**

PROHIBITIONS

I'd rather you didn't go.
You may not go.
Please don't go.
Don't go.
I won't allow you to go.

You are forbidden to go.
You'd better not go.
I forbid you to go.
I wouldn't go if I were you.
You mustn't go.

Command	Direct prohibition	Indirect prohibition	Request

FILL IN THE BLANKS

Verb	Noun	Adjective
		compulsory
	necessity	
expect		
oblige		
	force	
		permissible
object		
	refusal	
		authorised
agree		
	choice	
		selective
accept		
		avoided
reject		

SELECTION VERBS

● Put these verbs into the tree diagram below. Then compare these with your own language.

avoid
choose
decline
demand
insist on
pick
prefer
refuse
select
turn down

```
                    ┌────── selection ──────┐
            acceptance                non-acceptance
         ┌──────┴──────┐           ┌──────┴──────┐
      verbal      non-verbal     verbal      non-verbal
     ........    ..........    ..........   ..........
     ........    ..........    ..........
                 ..........    ..........
                 ..........
```

TEST YOURSELF ● Listen to the passage being read to you. Then read the questions below. Listen to the passage again before writing your answers in the boxes.

1 Easter Island was discovered by—
   a a Norwegian
   b Chile
   c Thor Heyerdahl
   d a Dutchman

2 It was discovered in the .... century.
   a 16th
   b 17th
   c 18th
   d 19th

3 The island belongs to—
   a Chile
   b Peru
   c Holland
   d Norway

4 The first people to live on the island arrived—
   a a thousand years ago
   b two thousand years ago
   c with their gods
   d with huge stone statues

5 More than 1000 huge stone statues .... on the island.
   a stand upright
   b exist
   c have fallen
   d are 9 metres tall

6 The stone statues—
   a are over 2000 years old
   b came on the Kon-Tiki
   c were carved by the original inhabitants
   d came from S. America.

7 The island is called Easter Island because—
   a it was discovered on Easter Day
   b it has huge stone statues
   c it lies to the East of other islands
   d the first inhabitants came from the East

8 Kon-Tiki was the name of—
   a an ocean current
   b a Pacific island
   c a Norwegian explorer
   d a wooden raft

9 Heyerdahl is—
   a Norwegian
   b Dutch
   c Peruvian
   d Chilean

10 Heyerdahl proved that—
   a the islanders came from S. America
   b the islanders could have come from S. America
   c other islands lie to the West
   d the island is to the West of S. America

Unit 4

CUED DIALOGUE

Situation   Two friends talking at a party.

References: C1, C2

A invites B's opinion of C's appearance.
B makes non-committal comment.
A disapproves of C's clothes.

B agrees.
A repeats disapproval.
B agrees.

B disagrees and offers own approval.
A presses for confirmation.
B approves again with evidence.

A admires C's character, however.
B agrees.

ANNUAL STAFF APPRAISAL

Please attend at .... on .... at the Personnel Office for your annual appraisal.

The questions below are designed to help you prepare for the interview in an honest and thoughtful way. You need not bring this form with you to the appraisal, and you need not complete it if you prefer not to.

Personal qualities

On careful reflection I believe I am: hardworking / conscientious / fairly conscientious / undisciplined / lazy

With my colleagues I am: outgoing / friendly / restrained / detached / withdrawn

When changes are suggested, I am: flexible / open-minded / quite adaptable / set in my ways / inflexible

I want my superiors to think I am: dynamic / enthusiastic / active / laid back / indifferent

Privately, I know I am: dynamic / enthusiastic / active / laid back / indifferent

Motivation and attitude to work

I approach my job with: keenness / interest / tolerance / indifference / hatred

I regard the company with: devotion / loyalty / sympathy / indifference / hatred

I would change my job: at the earliest opportunity / readily / if necessary / reluctantly / under no circumstances

I am .... suited to my job.   completely / well / reasonably / only partially / in no way

I am .... to take a more senior position.   ambitious / agreeable / prepared / not anxious / unwilling

Professional qualities

My punctuality is: excellent / good / average / fair / poor

I have been absent during the last year: very frequently / often / occasionally / rarely / never

As a member of a team I am: fully cooperative / helpful / usually helpful / uncooperative / obstructive

I believe I am .... for my job.   over-qualified / well qualified / qualified / underqualified / unqualified

I am .... to take further training.   keen / willing / prepared / reluctant / unwilling

STEPPING STONES

JUNIOR ASSISTANT

Required by mail order department handling offers for *Cosmopolitan, Good Housekeeping, Harpers & Queen* and other quality magazines.

Applicants should have at least four 'O' levels, one of which must be English. The successful candidate will be bright, enthusiastic, with an excellent telephone manner and enjoy dealing with people. Good typing essential as is the ability to write own letters. WP experience would be an advantage. IBM-PC preferred. Ideal position for 2nd jobber.

Please apply by hand-written letter enclosing current CV, stating present salary and availability to **Beverlie Flower, The National Magazine Co. Ltd., National Magazine House, 72 Broadwick St., London, W1V 2BP.**

ADMIN ASSISTANT
C £8,000

We are a small but growing retail business.

We require an intelligent and numerate person with typing and book keeping skills capable of working unsupervised.

If you are responsible, have initiative and the personality to fit in with a bright and energetic team phone Georgina Sant on **581 2058** now!

The Sleeping Company

123 Fulham Road   London SW3 6RT

PERSONAL QUALITIES

● Write the opposites of the following adjectives in the columns on the right.

active	loyal
adequate	modest
agreeable	moral
contented	sane
cooperative	sociable
elegant	sympathetic
enthusiastic	tidy
honest	tolerant

un-	in-	im-	dis-

● Write the adjectives below in the correct squares.

of men

of women

attractive	smart
chic	striking
handsome	ugly
plain	untidy
pretty	

1 Victoria Cross, awarded to officers and men of all 3 services for 'conspicuous bravery or devotion to their country in the presence of the enemy'. The highest honour.

2 George Cross, mainly for civilians of Britain and the British Commonwealth; awarded for valour and outstanding gallantry displayed under dangerous conditions. The second highest honour.

3 Distinguished Service Order, awarded to officers of all the armed forces for distinguished service in war.

4 Distinguished Service Cross, awarded to officers of the Royal Navy, Royal Marines and Womens' Royal Naval Service for gallant and distinguished conduct.

5 Military Cross, awarded to Army Officers and Warrant Officers for gallant and distinguished service in action.

6 Distinguished Flying Cross, awarded to officers and Warrant Officers of the Royal Air Force for valour, gallantry and devotion to duty while flying.

1

2

3

4

5

6

WHAT GOES WITH WHAT?

	man	woman	idea	plan	writer	book
clever						
intelligent						
brainy						
brilliant						
bright						
wise						
sensible						
able						
skilful						
proficient						
talented						
gifted						

FOR TRANSLATION

His face was as white as a sheet.
She's as brown as a berry.
The baby's as good as gold.
She looked as pretty as a picture.
They are as thick as thieves.

Her face went as red as a beetroot.
He stood there as cool as a cucumber.
I'm fine thanks: as fit as a fiddle.
He looked as strong as an ox.
He is as thick as two short planks.

TEST YOURSELF ● Listen to the passage being read to you. It has ten missing words. Choose the best word in each case from the words given below, and draw a line under the word you choose.

1 met	joined	arrived	entered
2 loyalty	friendship	trust	support
3 disappointed	unhappy	saddened	reluctant
4 generosity	reliance	truth	loyalty
5 judgement	acceptance	confidence	belief
6 helpful	kind	generous	good
7 amiable	easy	close	human
8 glad	happy	delighted	jolly
9 tidy	pleasing	charming	nice
10 expensive	valuable	glorious	terrific

Unit 5

CUED DIALOGUE

Situation   Interview for a job.

References: A8, A11, B1, C12, C15, C20, L1.4

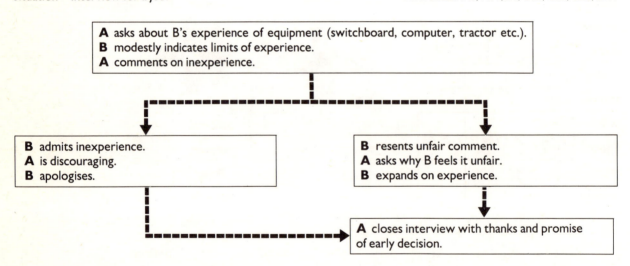

WHAT GOES WITH WHAT?

	John	the time	computers	Chinese
Do you know				
Have you any knowledge of				
Do you understand				
Have you any understanding of				
Do you recognise				
Are you conscious of				
Are you aware of				
Are you familiar with				
Are you acquainted with				
Are you conversant with				

STARTER STUDIO FLAT

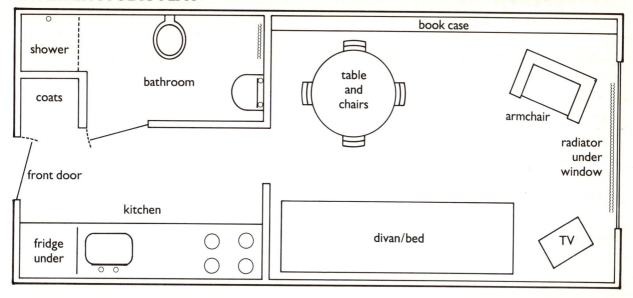

DEGREES OF CERTAINTY

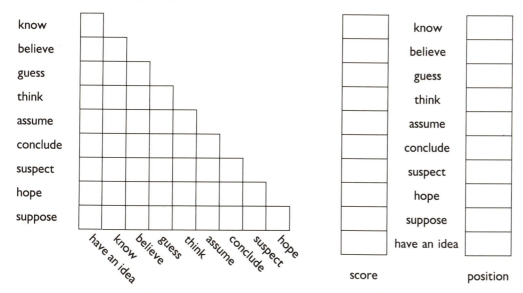

FILL IN THE BLANKS

Noun	Adjective	Verb
	known	
		ignore
student		
		reason
		argue
	believable	
criticism		
		comprehend
information		
	theoretical	

WAYS OF THINKING ● Draw lines from the verbs to the nouns.

calculate	priest
conclude	valuer
imagine	novelist
estimate	engineer
guess	judge
believe	detective
assess	gambler
interpret	art critic
reason	philosopher
judge	astronaut

TEST YOURSELF ● Listen to the passage being read to you. It has ten missing words. Choose the best word in each case from the words given below, and draw a line under the word you choose.

1	taught	preached	coached	educated
2	what	which	whom	that
3	for	to	from	of
4	round	along	within	for
5	against	about	with	from
6	over	contrary	with	against
7	middle	centre	heart	inside
8	doubted	denied	refused	criticised
9	demanded	criticised	commanded	insisted
10	refused	denied	doubted	disbelieved

Unit 6

CUED DIALOGUE

Situation Neighbours meet.   *References*: A6, A9, A11, C7, C9, C12, L2.4.4/7/13

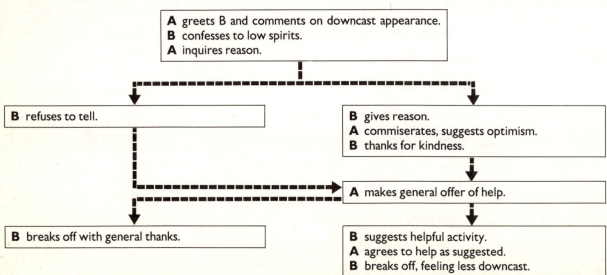

FOR TRANSLATION

1 The new submarine can dive and remain underwater without surfacing for up to ten weeks.
2 The sun rises in the east and sets in the west.
3 Metals expand when heated and contract again when the temperature falls.
4 STOL identifies planes which can take off and land on short runways.
5 Modern photocopiers can enlarge and reduce originals.
6 The tides ebb and flow under the influence of the moon.
7 Press the accelerator pedal and the engine speeds up: release the pedal and the engine slows down.
8 At the end of the football season, the most successful clubs are promoted to a higher division and the least successful are relegated.
9 In general hospitals most patients are usually improving, but in geriatric hospitals most are deteriorating.
10 Before each race the jockeys mount their horses before leaving the enclosure and do not dismount until they have returned to it.

HOW MUCH LIQUID?

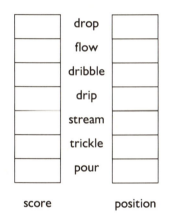

RISE AND FALL

● Complete the sentences below with appropriate words from the list provided.

1 The .... in the inflation rate is only temporary.
2 The .... of a flag to half-mast is a sign of mourning.
3 The first .... of Mount Everest was made in 1953.
4 A photographer can make an .... of a picture.
5 The .... of the school leaving age should improve standards.
6 The discovery of oil is a great .... to a nation's economy.
7 Every government is delighted at an .... in exports.
8 An .... in one's salary is usually welcome.
9 A plane's .... after take-off can be a dangerous period.
10 Churchill turned down an .... to the peerage.

upsurge
climb
elevation
ascent
increase
rise
swelling
enlargement
raising
boost
hoisting
jump

WHAT GOES WITH WHAT?

	value	price	business	speed	size	popularity	accident numbers	national average
decrease								
fall								
drop								
reduction								
collapse								
slump								
dip								
dive								
plunge								
cut								

● Do the same in your mother tongue.

FILL IN THE BLANKS

Noun	Adjective	Verb
		multiply
		condense
reduction		
reinforcement		
	collapsed	
	swollen	
		submerge
enlargement		
	shed	
		overthrow

TEST YOURSELF ● Listen to the passage being read to you. It has ten missing words. Choose the best word in each case from the words given below and draw a line under the word you choose.

1	raising	longing	spreading	extending
2	reduced	shortened	abridged	declined
3	released	robbed	free	unaware
4	made	introduced	gained	raised
5	insured	protected	covered	free
6	clear	certain	safe	sure
7	met	sprouted	grew	developed
8	started	entered	initialled	opened
9	spread	expanded	broadened	accelerated
10	lost	went	disappeared	vanished

Unit 7

CUED DIALOGUES

He draws attention to large crate.
She expresses amusement at secret joke about crate.
He doesn't see any joke.
She asks him to photograph her on crate.
He doubts her ability to mount it.
She (on crate) makes him wait until she's in the right position. Then gives him the OK.

He doesn't see the point.
She tells him to wait to see photo.

He sees joke through camera view-finder.
Compliments her.
She thanks him.

She draws attention to large crate.
He thinks it will make a good snapshot.
She doesn't see why.
He asks if she would climb up onto crate.
She agrees to try, and succeeds.
He poses her.

She ridicules pose.
He promises explanation soon.
She (on ground) sees joke, is amused.
He hopes picture comes out well.

She sees the joke. Is amused.
He promises her a copy.
She insists on taking his photo next.
He objects, can't be called 'lass'.
She explains he'll stand in front of crate with his head obscuring the 'GL'.

FOR TRANSLATION

a a strong man   a strongbox   strong drink   having a strong head   strong language   strong minded   my strong point   a strong-room   strong verbs   still going strong

b a weak man   weak-headed   weak-hearted   weak-kneed   weak-minded

c power plant   a power point   power politics   in power   the powers that be

WORLD FUEL AND ENERGY ● Complete the pie charts.

● **Nuclear energy**
The first source of nuclear power was developed in Britain in 1956. Energy is obtained from heat generated by the reaction from splitting atoms of certain elements, of which uranium and plutonium are the most important. Although the initial installation costs are very high the actual running costs are low.

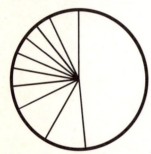

48% U.S.A., 9% U.K. Japan,
6% W. Germany, 4% Canada Sweden
France, 3.5% U.S.S.R., 2.5% Belgium,
10% Others

▽ **Coal**
Once the most important source of power, coal's importance now lies in the production of electricity and as a raw material in the production of plastics, heavy chemicals and disinfectants.

▲ **Oil**
It is a complex mixture of hydrocarbons which are refined to extract the various constituents. These include products such as gasolene, kerosene and heavy fuel oils. Oil is rapidly replacing coal because of easier handling and reduced pollution.

■ **Natural gas**
Since the early 1960's natural gas (methane) has become one of the largest single sources of energy. By liquefaction its volume can be reduced to 1/600 of that of gas and hence is easily transported. Because it is both cheaper than coal gas and less polluting it has great potential.

□ **Water**
Hydro-electric power stations use water to drive turbines which in turn generate electricity. The ideal site is one in which a consistently large volume of water falls a considerable height, hence sources of H.E.P. are found mainly in mountainous areas.

 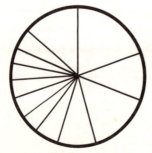 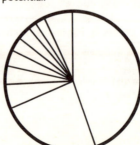 

25% U.S.A., 21% U.S.S.R., 20% China, 7.5% Poland, 5% U.K., 4% India, 3.5% W. Germ. S. Afr., 3% Australia, 1% Czechoslavakia, 6.5% Others

20% U.S.S.R., 15% U.S.A., 14% Saudi Arabia, 9% Iran, 4.5% Iraq, 4% Libya Kuwait Venezuela, 3.5% Nigeria, 3% China U.A.E., 16% Others

43% U.S.A., 25% U.S.S.R., 6.5% Netherlands, 5.5% Canada, 3% U.K. Rumania, 2% Iran, 1.5% W. Germany, 1% Mexico, 9.5% Others

21% U.S.S.R., 18% U.S.A., 14% Canada, 5.5% Japan, 5% Norway Brazil, 3.5% Sweden, 3% France, 2.5% Italy, 22.5% Others

> DYNAMIC young graduate with strengths in German, Japanese and word processing seeks change. Confident, loyal and good sense of humour. Willing to travel.

NOW SELL YOURSELF
(1) lively / energetic / bright / intelligent
(2) young / mature
(3) manageress / administrator / personal assistant
(4) gifted / talented / outstanding
(5) secretarial / managerial / administrative
(6) positive / optimistic / confident
(7) willing / ready / eager / keen
(8) loyalty / commitment

(1).................... (2)....................
(3).................... seeks new position.
(4).................... linguist with (5).................... skills and (6).................... outlook. (7).................... to travel and give total (8)....................

VERBS ENDING IN -EN

....
....
....

VERBS STARTING IN EN-

....
....
....

TEST YOURSELF ● Listen to the passage being read to you. It has ten missing words. Choose the best word in each case from the words given below and draw a line under the word you choose.

1 frequent	common	regular	ordinary
2 amassing	assembling	finding	collecting
3 strength	force	heat	might
4 reflect	transmit	shoot	project
5 drove	crossed	overran	overcame
6 speed	pace	rate	velocity
7 up-to-date	topically	recently	currently
8 made	manufactured	found	produced
9 toured	voyaged	journeyed	travelled
10 plenty	surplus	enough	extra

Unit 8

CUED DIALOGUE
Situation   Runner seeks support for sponsored run.

| **A** greets B. Mentions his/her forthcoming sponsored run. |

| **B** returns greeting, cool about run.
A enthuses about run — when, where.
B scorns sponsoring.
A explains benefit to charity.
B relents, agreeing minimal sponsorship. | **B** returns greeting requests details of run.
A enthuses, gives date, time, distances.
B asks what is expected of sponsors.
A explains.
B agrees to sponsor modestly. |

| **A** thanks and says goodbye. |

MOVEMENT VERBS

● Write the following verbs in the appropriate parts of the diagram. Some can only take place on land, on the sea or in the air, some apply to two and some apply to three elements.

climb	drift	ride	swim
cruise	float	sail	tow
dance	fly	sink	transport
descend	march	ski	travel
dive	return	submerge	walk

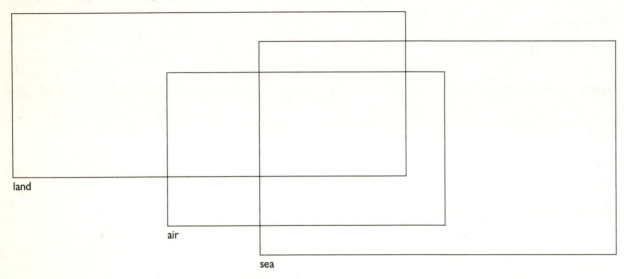

FOR TRANSLATION

The engine is running.   My nose is running.   I'm running short of money.
Who's running in the election?   She's running a shop.   She's running a temperature.
We visited London three years running.   The clock has run down.   I feel run down.
He's having a run of bad luck.

RUNNING AND WALKING

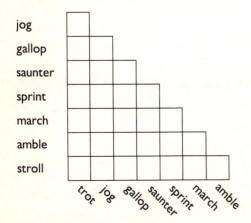

score   position

INTERESTING IDIOMS

break ....
....
catch ....
....
come ....
....
get ....
....
go ....
....
have ....
....
pull ....
....
put ....
....
take ....
....

WHAT GOES WITH WHAT?

	hands	head	eyes	tail	arms	a finger	a foot
shake							
wave							
blink							
nod							
wag							
open							
swing							
tap							
fold							
cross							

TEST YOURSELF ● Listen to the passage being read to you. It has ten missing words. Choose the best word in each case from the words given below and draw a line under the word you choose.

1	got	went	arrived	travelled
2	went	got	sounded	ran
3	questioned	queried	wondered	decided
4	covered	crossed	cut	transfixed
5	met	encountered	found	worked out
6	slight	thin	fine	narrow
7	brightening	glistening	smouldering	burning
8	climb	clamber	scramble up	escalate
9	enclosed	sandwiched	squeezed	surrounded
10	arrived	walked	run	gone

Unit 9

CUED DIALOGUE

Situation Two old friends meet.

References: C1, C7, C8, C10, C12, C27, L1.5.5/6, L1.6.1/2

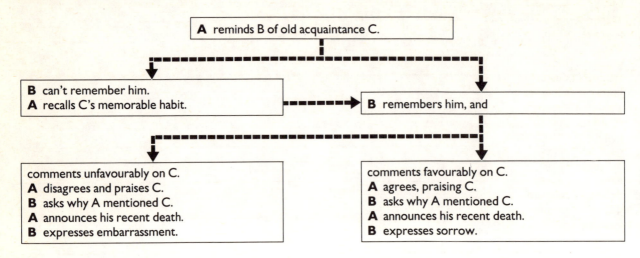

FOR TRANSLATION

Let's hear from you.   *Get in touch.*

Give us a [buzz. / ring. / call.]   Drop us a [note. / line. / card.]   [Call / Drop / Pop] in when you can.

COMMUNICATION VERBS

advise
announce
answer
chat
correspond
declare
explain
gossip
inform
mutter
print
pronounce

question
reply
say
scribble
state
talk
tell
threaten
utter
warn
whisper
write

speech

writing

VERBS BECOME NOUNS ● Change the verbs below into nouns by writing them in the spaces on the right with the correct ending.

accuse	express
admit	guide
agree	inform
allege	inquire
approve	insist
argue	judge
assess	mock
assume	object
betray	observe
condemn	oppose
confess	publish
confide	recommend
declare	refuse
deliver	remit
deny	repeat
detect	tolerate
discuss	transmit
educate	try

...........................al .... ance ....ation
...........................al .... ance ....ation
...........................al .... ence ....ation
...........................al .... ence ....ation
...........................al .... ition ....ation
...........................ery .... ition ....ation
...........................y .... ssion ....ation
...........................y .... ssion ....ation
.... ment .... ssion ....ation
.... ment .... ssion ....ation
.... ment .... ssion .... ion
.... ment .... ssion .... ion
                                 .... ption

COMMUNICATION IDIOMS ● Complete these five idioms, then draw lines to join them with their meanings.

Spinning a ....   Deceiving

Letting the cat out of the ....   Lying

Picking somebody's ....   Revealing a secret

Leading somebody up the garden ....   Reassuring

Setting somebody's mind at ....   Learning from somebody

TEST YOURSELF ● Listen to the passage being read to you. It has ten missing words. Choose the best word in each case from the words given below and draw a line under the word you choose.

1	talk	communicate	chat	correspond
2	say	speak	declare	announce
3	discovered	realised	observed	looked at
4	meaning	understanding	information	news
5	study	detective	investigation	search
6	supposed	remarked	knew	discovered
7	knew	calculated	found	remarked
8	realised	wondered	questioned	misunderstood
9	informed	told	printed	transmitted
10	thoughts	theories	communication	information

Unit 10

CUED DIALOGUES

Situation Travelling salesman and customer.

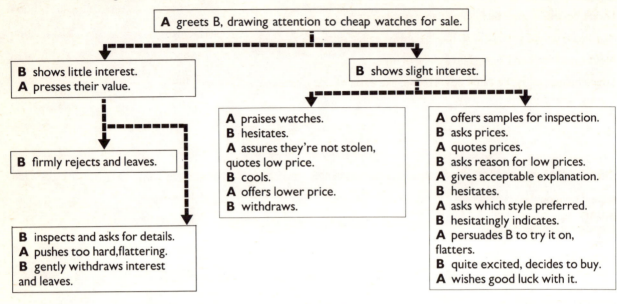

```
                A greets B, drawing attention to cheap watches for sale.
                                    |
       ┌────────────────────────────┴────────────────────────────┐
       ▼                                                         ▼
B shows little interest.                              B shows slight interest.
A presses their value.                                          │
       │                                          ┌─────────────┴─────────────┐
       ▼                                          ▼                           ▼
B firmly rejects and leaves.              A praises watches.         A offers samples for inspection.
       │                                  B hesitates.               B asks prices.
       │                                  A assures they're not      A quotes prices.
       │                                    stolen, quotes low price. B asks reason for low prices.
       ▼                                  B cools.                   A gives acceptable explanation.
B inspects and asks for details.          A offers lower price.      B hesitates.
A pushes too hard, flattering.            B withdraws.               A asks which style preferred.
B gently withdraws interest                                          B hesitatingly indicates.
  and leaves.                                                        A persuades B to try it on,
                                                                       flatters.
                                                                     B quite excited, decides to buy.
                                                                     A wishes good luck with it.
```

DIFFERENCES OF OPINION ● The following words all mean some kind of an opinion. Use them, once each, in the following sentences.

advice   assessment   decision   interpretation   theory
appreciation attitude   diagnosis   judgement   verdict

1 Doctors usually need to examine a patient before giving a ....
2 Juries consider the evidence in private before reaching their ....
3 'According to my .... ,' the valuer said, 'this antique is worthless.'
4 Saint Paul expresses a favourable .... towards wine.
5 'My .... ,' the judge told the prisoner, 'is that you go to prison.'
6 Critics occasionally write a warm .... of a new novel.
7 Scientists often research for years before proposing a new ....
8 Palmists give you an .... of the lines on your hand.
9 Football referees signal their .... by a whistle and gestures.
10 Most children live to regret not listening to their parents' sound ....

MAKING UP YOUR MIND ● What do you look for?

Buying clothes   *Buying food*   *Buying a car*

good price   good material   cheap   expensive   fast   noisy
good name   good fit   fresh   tastes good   dangerous   beautiful
good colour   good design   good colour   easy to prepare   expensive   makes my friends
                                                               cheap to run   jealous
                                                               foreign   makes the girls
                                                                               like me

● Which criteria are (il)logical, (un)scientific, (un)reasonable, (in)appropriate?

IDIOMS RELATING TO GIVING OPINIONS
● Finish these idioms.

Don't beat about the .... , come straight to the point.

I don't believe a word he said, he's always shooting a ....

You know where you are with him, he always calls a spade a ....

Next time I see him I'll give him a piece of my ....

I think he was angry: he came down on me like a ton of ....

DECISION MAKING ● We reach decisions as the result of:

expert opinion
flattery
friendly recommendation
gossip
guesswork
intuition
logic
personal experience
scientific evidence
statistics
trusted advice
written evidence
etc.

● Write this onto the scale below.

subjective ←--→ objective

....

    ....

TEST YOURSELF ● Listen to the passage being read to you. It has ten missing words. Choose the best word in each case from the words given below and draw a line under the word you choose.

1 lesson	opinion	principle	theme
2 concept	verdict	thought	view
3 assume	suggest	consent	believe
4 refused	denied	forbidden	disapproved
5 permitted	let	approved	agreed
6 believers	seconders	supporters	enthusiasts
7 reject	avoid	lose	miss
8 campaign	plot	plan	operation
9 unfriendly	disapproving	hostile	mistrusting
10 accept	consent	support	approve

Unit 11

CUED DIALOGUES

Situation Two friends meet after some time.

References: A9, B1, B3, C3, C4

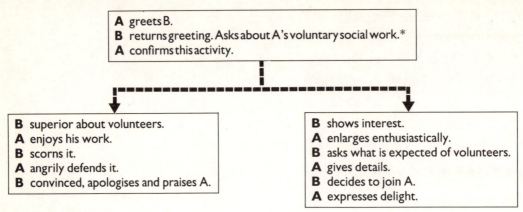

A greets B.
B returns greeting. Asks about A's voluntary social work.*
A confirms this activity.

B superior about volunteers.
A enjoys his work.
B scorns it.
A angrily defends it.
B convinced, apologises and praises A.

B shows interest.
A enlarges enthusiastically.
B asks what is expected of volunteers.
A gives details.
B decides to join A.
A expresses delight.

* Suggested openings:
What's all this about you doing ...
Is it really true that you're ...
A little bird told me you're doing ...
They tell me ...
I hear ...

EXHAUSTION ADJECTIVES ● Consider this list of English adjectives.
Some can only be used with living things (people, animals), some only with non-living things, and some can be used with both. Write each word in the appropriate part of the diagram below.

exhausted   stale
fatigued   tired
listless   weary
sleepy   worn out

living

non-living

● Do the same thing with words of similar meaning in your own language.

FIXED SIMILES ● Complete the following English fixed similes with the name of an animal, bird or insect. Then translate into your own language for comparison. How many animals etc. do you use?

as blind as a ....

as crafty as a ....

as gentle as a ....

as playful as a ....

as proud as a ....

as busy as a ....

as fat as a ....

as mad as a ....

as stubborn as a ....

as quiet as a ....

INCREASING AND DECREASING VERBS ● Complete the following sentences using the appropriate form of pairs of verbs.

↑ means the verb has a notion of increasing
↓ means the verb has a notion of decreasing

1 ↓ a mountain usually takes less time than ↑ .

2 Some woollen clothes ↑ when they are washed; others ↓ .

3 As medical knowledge has ↑ the numbers of child deaths have ↓ .

4 Metals ↑ in higher temperatures and ↓ in lower ones.

5 In the N. Hemisphere, days ↑ and nights ↓ as midsummer approaches.

6 Modern photocopiers can ↓ originals or ↑ them.

7 If our body temperature ↑ too high or ↓ too low, it shows we are ill.

8 The more care we put into our work, the more it ↑ ; the less care, the more our work ↓ .

9 A powerful engine helps a car ↑ very quickly: it needs powerful brakes to ↓ equally quickly.

10 Honesty can only ↑ a friendship; dishonesty always ↓ it.

ODD MAN OUT ● One of the nouns on the left cannot be the subject of the verb on the right. Identify the odd man out.

colour	noise	light	hope	courage	ambition	distance	**fade**
a person	a building	a business	a stone	optimism	a tent	one's health	**collapse**
a rope	speed	electricity	rain	a storm	inflation	activity	**slacken**
a ship	a stone	one's face	the sun	one's heart	one's spirits	a lift	**sink**
a person	a plant	a business	a noise	anger	a photograph	love	**grow**
a road	a noise	one's finger	wood	one's heart	one's head		**swell**
metal	one's chest	population	trade	rubber	noise	a chain of shops	**expand**
grass	disease	a rod	a population	a city	one's hands	excitement	**spread**

FOR TRANSLATION

a rain drops   chocolate drops   at the drop of a hat   the penny dropped
   you could hear a pin drop   a drop in the ocean   to drop a brick   to drop behind
   to drop a hint   to drop in on someone   to drop off   to drop out   a drop-out

b a waterfall   rainfall   nightfall   fall-out   to fall out   to fall behind   to fall in love
   to fall on one's feet   to fall out with someone
   to fall over backwards to help someone   to fall short   to fall through

c a face-lift   a fork-lift truck   a ski-lift   a tail-lift   a weight-lifter   a shop-lifter
   we have lift-off   a lift shaft   the mist lifted   she doesn't lift a finger   to thumb a lift

TEST YOURSELF ● Listen to the passage being read to you. It has ten missing words. Choose the best word in each case from the lists below, and underline your choice.

1 raised	expanded	extended	developed
2 reducing	dropping	lowering	falling
3 spread	extended	prolonged	magnified
4 expanded	spread	stretched	amplified
5 trickle	sink	flow	swell
6 collecting	creating	producing	having
7 rises	lifts	climbs	ascends
8 heightens	builds	expands	stretches
9 drops	sinks	drips	pours
10 rushes	moves	trickles	drifts

Unit 12

CUED DIALOGUES

Situation   Interviewer and passer-by in street.

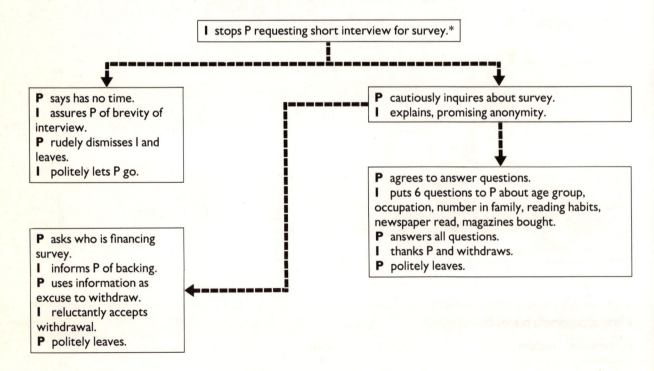

* Suggested formulae:
   Could you let me have just a few seconds to ask you some questions?
   Could you spare (me) a few moments of your time?
   Would you mind taking part in a public survey?
   Have you got a couple of free moments to answer a few questions?

FOR TRANSLATION

a a throw-away lighter   to throw a party   to throw a spanner in the works
to throw in the towel   to throw light upon a problem   to throw one's hand in
to throw oneself at someone   to throw someone off the scent
to throw something out of gear   to throw one's weight about

b to recover one's sight   to recover consciousness   to recover one's health
to recover lost time   to recover one's balance   to make a speedy recovery
to recover a lost possession   to recover one's investment
to recover a wreck from the seabed

c waste ground   a waste pipe   waste products   to go to waste
don't waste your breath   waste not, want not   to lay waste to a city
what a waste of time   a wasting disease   don't waste your money

WHAT'S THE DIFFERENCE?
● Put these words into phrases to show the difference in meaning.

dismantle	remnant	salvage	remainder	cast-off
remains	castaway	demolish	residue	scavenge

VERBS BECOME NOUNS ● Write the noun forms of the following verbs in the appropriate places on the right.

contaminate	reclaim	..........................ation	..........................age
demolish	recover		
dispose	reject	..........................ation	..........................age
drain	renew		
leak	waste	..........................ition	..........................age
pollute	wreck		
		..........................ution	..........................age
		..........................ion	..........................al
		..........................y	..........................al

WHAT GOES WITH WHAT?

	food	paper	cloth	wine
scrap				
crumb				
remnant				
remains				
dregs				

● Do the same with your own language.

WORDS STARTING WITH Re–
● The following words are taken from the article on p48. *Re–* means 'again'. Write definitions, using 'again', for these and other words beginning with *re–*.

retrain.. ....

return.. ....

recycle.. ....

resale.. ....

reclamation... ....

re-use... ....

TEST YOURSELF ● Listen to the passage being read to you. It has ten missing words. Choose the best word in each case from the lists below and underline your choice.

1	variety	variation	alternative	difference
2	thrown	squandered	wasted	disposed
3	rash	unnecessary	wasteful	pitiful
4	disposal	redundant	drained	rid
5	tips	heaps	dumps	hills
6	wrecks	spoils	damages	demolishes
7	give	have	provide	produce
8	form	generate	cause	produce
9	manufactures	makers	reasons	sources
10	fumes	smoke	clouds	smells

Unit 13

CUED DIALOGUES

Situation Customer and salesman.

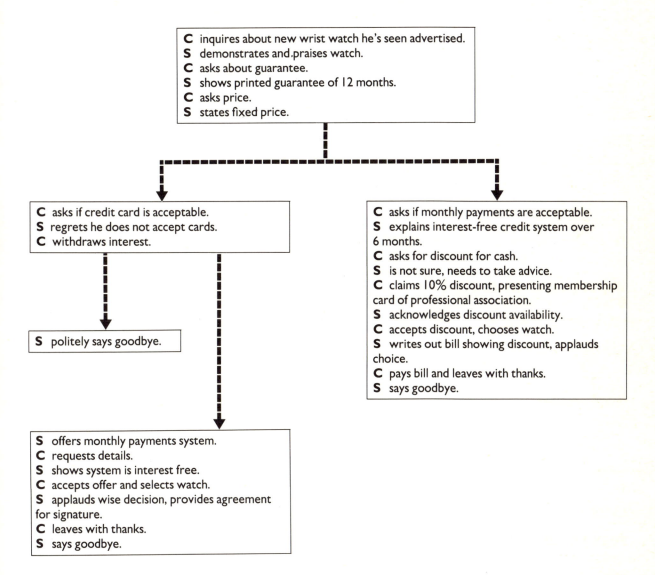

JUMBLED DEFINITIONS ● Write the ten following nouns in the boxes alongside the appropriate definitions.

catalogue   draft   plan   project   schedule
design   itinerary   programme   prospectus syllabus

☐	descriptive notice of series of events, intended sequence of proceedings: as for a concert, radio and TV transmissions, course of study etc.
☐	plan for and listed details of a journey, or route: issued by travel agent or tour organiser
☐	complete list, often with descriptions and other particulars: issued by mail order firms, sale rooms, libraries etc.
☐	list of details in table form, often giving proposed times: timetable for airlines, for an important visit or event
☐	printed outline giving details of and advertising something: describing a college, forthcoming book, a new business enterprise etc.
☐	drawing, outline or scheme from which something can be made: used at the planning stage for gardens, clothes, theatre sets and most man-made objects
☐	outline drawing diagram showing relative sizes and positions as seen from above: of a building, city centre, garden, large machine
☐	scheme, or undertaking: a single undertaking lasting, for instance, a school term; a government scheme etc.
☐	outline or summary of contents of a course of study: description of a school or college subject
☐	rough outline of something to be done: first sketch of a speech, letter, piece of legislation etc.

FOR TRANSLATION

a a sign   a signboard   a signpost   sign-writing   a sign of the times
the sign of the cross   to sign one's name   to sign off   to sign on   a good sign
a rude sign   a road sign

b a design   a school of design   graphic design   whether by accident or design
to have designs on someone   by design   computer assisted design (CAD)
a fashion designer   a designing man/woman

A SALES GRAPH
● Travel agent's bookings? Umbrella sales? Tennis racket sales?

WORDS STARTING WITH Pre—

● *Pre—* carries the meaning 'before in time', 'in advance', 'beforehand'. Use one of these meanings in writing definitions of the following.

precedent ....
predestination ....
predict ....
prejudice ....
premature ....
preparatory ....
prevent ....
preview ....
previous ....
pre-war ....

WHAT GOES WITH WHAT?

	food	drink	flowers	clothes	taxi	theatre seat	train seat	plane ticket	hotel room	long distance call	tennis court	restaurant table	letter	car	student
order															
book															
reserve															
register															

TEST YOURSELF

● Listen to the passage being read to you. There are ten spaces in it as usual. But this time, three of the four words in each list will fill the space (though they may not have exactly the same meaning). You must cross out the unacceptable word.

1	decided	thought	planned	concluded
2	plan	thing	idea	prospect
3	work	appointment	job	post
4	flinging	throwing	sending	tossing
5	undid	unfastened	opened	loosened
6	dropped	folded	arranged	placed
7	guess	foresee	imagine	anticipate
8	turned	pressed	put	switched
9	examined	stared	looked	glanced
10	upset	displeased	worried	anxious

Unit 14

CUED DIALOGUES

Situation Manager and assistant.

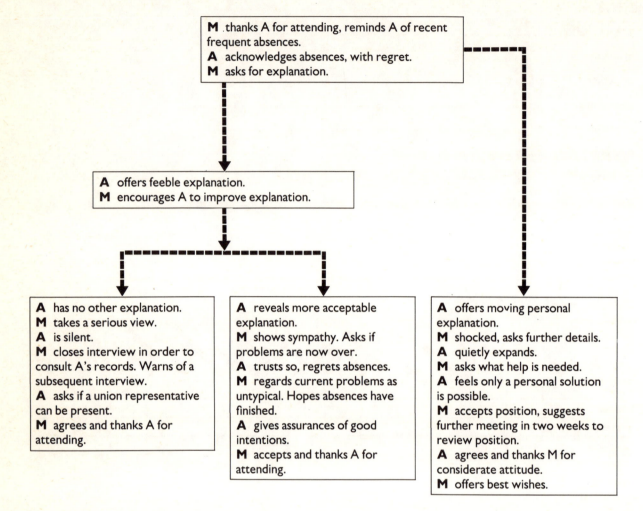

FOR TRANSLATION

to change   to change colour   to change money   to change hands
to change one's tune   to change the subject   to change one's mind
to change one's address   a change for the better   for a change   small change
a change of clothing   a change in the weather

● Translate to bring out the differences in meaning.

You must change those trousers.	You must alter those trousers.
They changed their shoes.	They exchanged their shoes.
I've changed my watch.	I've altered my watch.
It makes a change.	It makes a difference.
He's a changed man.	He's a new man.

OPPOSITES ● Complete each pair of verbs by adding the verb carrying the opposite meaning.

start	harden	raise	agree ....
.... go	.... darken	.... deteriorate	.... fail
add	shorten	increase	defend ....
.... depart	.... weaken	.... accelerate	.... encourage
accept	whiten	retreat	reject ....

VERBS BECOME NOUNS ● Change the verbs below into nouns by writing them in the spaces on the right, with the correct ending.

accept
amend
assist
convert
convey
develop
dismiss
disperse
encourage
enlarge
enter
explode
improve
limit
modify
move
produce
reduce
reform
refresh
refuse
remove
renew
reorganise
replace
resist
reverse
revive
transform
vary

........................ation   ....al
........................ation   ....al
........................ation   ....al
........................ation   ....al
........................ation   ....al
........................ation   ....al
........................sion   ....al
........................sion   ....ance
........................tion   ....ance
........................tion   ....ance
........................ment   ....ance
........................ment   ....ance
........................ment
........................ment
........................ment
........................ment
........................ment

IDIOMS RELATING TO CHANGE
● How would you translate these?

It's like water off a duck's back.

You can't teach an old dog new tricks.

A leopard never changes its spots.

TEST YOURSELF ● Listen to the passage being read to you. There are ten spaces in it. In each of the following lists three of the four words will fit the space (though they may not have exactly the same meaning). You should cross out the unacceptable word.

Notion

1	tossed	dropped	hurled	threw
2	examined	studied	inspected	viewed
3	familiar	notorious	well-known	recognisable
4	felt	disturbed	touched	handled
5	paused	interrupted	stopped	hesitated
6	cold	icy	chilled	frosty
7	catch	make out	discern	recognise
8	horrified	afraid	frightened	nervous
9	sent	pointed	aimed	directed
10	sure	certain	confident	secure

● Finally, try to identify the notion underlying the four alternative choices. For example, the four verbs in number one have in common the notion of 'sending by hand'.

Unit 15

CUED DIALOGUES

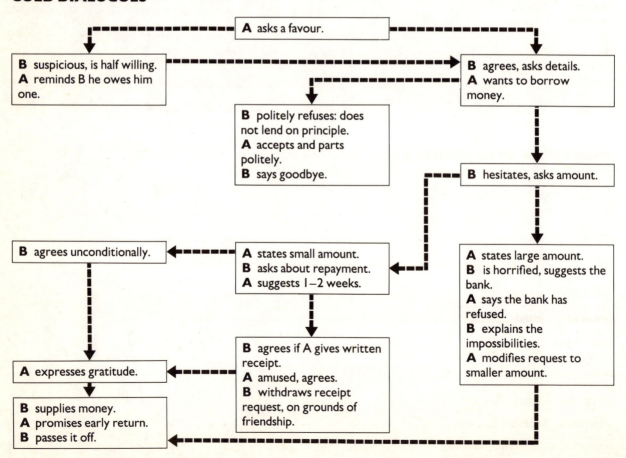

FOR TRANSLATION

a a stroke of a hammer   sun-stroke   breast-stroke   a stroke of the pen
   a stroke of luck   on the stroke of twelve   he never did a stroke of work

b to arrange a meeting   to arrange the furniture   to make arrangements
   future arrangements   flower arrangements   a musical arrangement
   an arranged marriage

c lead the way   lead astray   lead somebody a dance   lead somebody by the nose
   lead somebody up the garden path   lead a double life   lead a dog's life
   take the lead   a leading lady   a leading article   a leading question.

VERBS BECOME NOUNS ● Change the verbs below into nouns by writing them in the spaces with the correct ending.

administer	improve	.... ment	.......................ation	.......................ion
ally	inspire	.... ment	.......................ation	.......................ion
arrange	limit	.... ment	.......................ation	.......................ion
assure	manage	.... ment	.......................ation	.......................ion
confine	motivate	.... ment	.......................ation	.......................ion
correct	organise	.... ment	.......................ation	.......................ion
develop	permit	.... ment	.......................ation	.......................ion
dominate	persuade	.... ment	.... ance	.......................ion
excavate	punish	.... ment	.... ance	.......................ion
exclude	refresh	.... ment	.... ance	.......................ion
expand	regulate	.... ment	.... ance	.......................ion
govern	repress			.......................ion
guide	restore			.......................ion
impress	supervise			.......................ion
imprison	suppress			.......................ion

WHAT GOES WITH WHAT? ● All the ten verbs below mean 'control' in some way. Expand the lists of nouns appropriate to each verb.

fly	plane, ...
drive	train, ...
ride	horse, ...
conduct	orchestra, ...
govern	island, ...
command	ship, ...
manage	office, ...
direct	film, ...
supervise	workshop, ...
edit	TV programme, ...

IMPACT IDIOMS ● Complete the following idioms and translate them.

To rule the ....

To rule with a rod of ....

To keep under one's ....

To take the bull by the ....

To take the law into one's own ....

To put one's house in ....

To put one's .... down.

To put one's shoulder to the ....

To nip something in the ....

To hit the nail on the ....

TEST YOURSELF ● Listen to the passage being read to you. There are ten spaces in it. In each of the following lists three of the four words will fit the space (though they may not have exactly the same meaning). You should cross out the unacceptable word.

				Notion
1 remarkable	well-known	outstanding	notable	
2 growing	turning	approaching	becoming	
3 voyage	flight	trip	journey	
4 beginning	arrival	fall	onset	
5 stopped	prevented	prohibited	suppressed	
6 beat	exceed	outdo	break	
7 held up	detained	halted	arrested	
8 claimed	possessed	won	took	
9 exciting	melodramatic	stimulating	exhilarating	
10 believed	suspected	felt	declared	

● Finally, try to identify the notion underlying the four alternative choices and enter it in the right hand column.

Unit 16

CUED DIALOGUES

Situation Canvasser and voter.

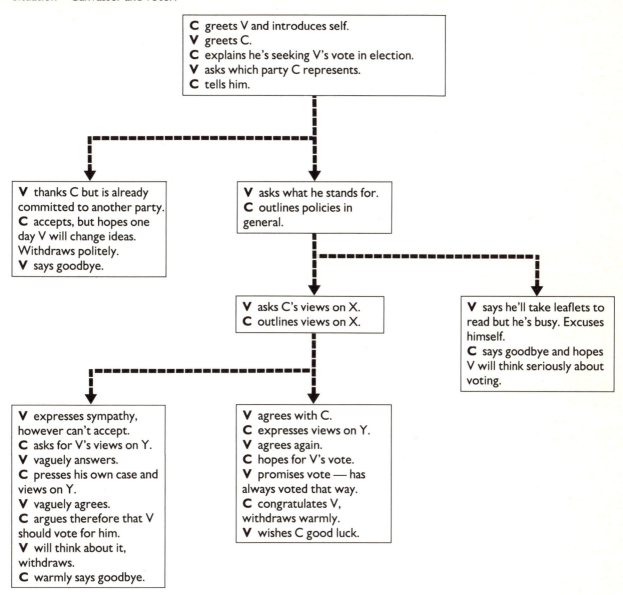

FOR TRANSLATION

a to join hands   to join forces with somebody   to join up   to join in   May I join you?
Will you join us in a drink?   Join the club!   out of joint
to put somebody's nose out of joint   a finger joint   a joint of meat   What a low joint!

b part-time   part-owner   to play a part   to take part in   for my part
a three-part serial   a spare part   a part of speech   to part with   to part one's hair
parting instructions   the parting of the ways

c a split vote   a split personality   a split second   a splitting headache
to split one's sides with laughter   to split hairs   to split the difference   to split up
to do the splits

DICTIONARY WORK ● Use your dictionary to complete these phrases.

Animates

a band of ....
a class of ....
a company of ....
a flock of ....
a gang of ....
a herd of ....
a litter of ....

a pack of ....
a school of ....
a shoal of ....
a swarm of ....
a team of ....
a troop of ....

Inanimates

a bunch of ....
a clump of ....
a crate of ....
a fleet of ....
a flight of ....
a pack of ....
a set of ....

WHAT'S THE DIFFERENCE? ● Explain, then translate.

She kept him in chains.	She kept him in ties.
He couldn't see the connection.	He couldn't see the junction.
The door is fastened.	The door is stuck.
He collects model aircraft.	He assembles model aircraft.
He trimmed his beard.	He cut off his beard.
Join the train at Crewe.	Meet the train at Crewe.
The lawyer put together his case.	The lawyer packed his case.
She's classifying flowers.	She's collecting flowers.
You need a connector.	You need a joiner.
The Redferns have moved.	The Redferns have separated.

JOINING IDIOMS ● Complete the following idioms and then translate them.

Birds of a feather .... together.

To put two and .... together.

To put your .... together.

To have one's .... tied.

To tie somebody in ....

To be tied to one's mother's ....

To meet somebody ....

To meet somebody's ....

To pull oneself ....

To pull one's ....

TEST YOURSELF ● Listen to the passage being read to you. There are ten spaces in it. In each of the following lists, three of the four words will fit the space (though they may not have exactly the same meaning). You should cross out the unacceptable word. Finally, add your idea of the notion.

					Notion
1	private	secret	confidential	concealed	
2	obstructed	interrupted	disturbed	troubled	
3	observe	watch	detect	examine	
4	colleague	workmate	companion	fellow	
5	heavy	onerous	oppressive	uncomfortable	
6	cover	conceal	hide	bury	
7	distinctly	obviously	plainly	clearly	
8	stepped	moved	trod	strode	
9	jabbed	punched	prodded	poked	
10	continue	remain	stay	keep	

Unit 17

CUED DIALOGUES

Situation Two people meet.

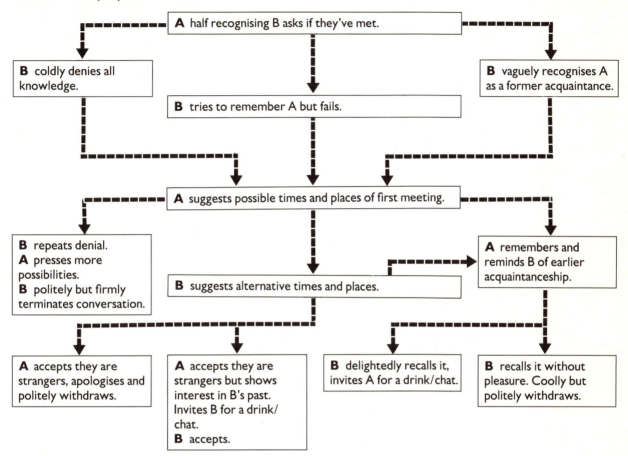

RECIPROCALS
● Several relationships are expressed in reciprocal pairs: parent/child, aunt/nephew etc. That is, if he is my parent, I am his child; if she is my aunt, I am her nephew. Think in what way to complete the pairs below.

....	niece	employer	....
wife	....	....	guest
....	captive	....	tenant
....	patient	....	victim
servant	....	teacher	....

● Think of verbs which are reciprocal (*buy/sell, borrow/lend*). Are there any reciprocal nouns and verbs in your own language which have no parallel in English, and vice versa?

FOR TRANSLATION

a on opposite sides   opposite angles   my opposite number   the people opposite
take the opposite view   in opposition   the leader of the opposition
the opposing team

b Help!   a home-help   mother's help   to give somebody a helping hand
to help oneself   self-help   So help me!   Not if I can help it
You can't help laughing   It can't be helped   Help me on/off with my coat, please

c freedom   a free agent   free and easy   free enterprise   free-fall   a free for all
a freelance writer   free-range eggs   a free thinker   to free-wheel

COMPARATIVE IDIOMS ● Complete, and then translate these idioms.

Like a bat out of ....   To sell like hot ....

To feel like a million ....   To spend money like ....

Like a red rag to a ....   Like water off a .... back.

Like father, like ....   Like two peas in a ....

Like .... I will.   Like nobody's ....

TEST YOURSELF ● Listen to the passage being read to you. There are ten spaces in it. In each of the following lists, three of the four words will fit the space (though they may not have exactly the same meaning). You should cross out the unacceptable word. Finally, add your idea of the notion.

				Notion
1 fairly	rather	kind of	quite	
2 becoming	flattering	enhancing	pale	
3 smooth	running	fluent	flowing	
4 bustle	excitement	interest	urgency	
5 persistently	constantly	forever	always	
6 combine	match	fit	couple	
7 felt	sensed	became aware	comprehended	
8 fixed	hooked	fastened	focused	
9 look	expression	gaze	view	
10 donated	presented	offered	awarded	

Unit 18

CUED DIALOGUES
Situation Salesman and customer.

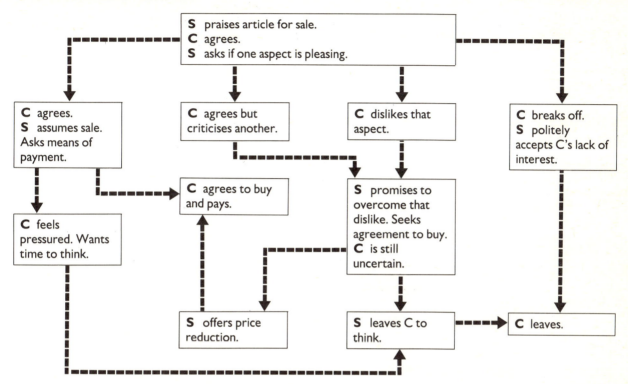

FOR TRANSLATION

a a stoppage   a stopper   a stop-cock   a stop-gap   a stop–go policy   a stop over   stop-press   a stop-watch   to pull out all the stops

b a starter (in a car)   a starter (first course)   a non-starter   a starting block   a starting gate   a starting pistol   the starting point   the starting price   to start something up   an upstart   a late starter   to get off to a good/bad start

c to go   to go ahead   to go in for something   to go off   to go one's own way   to go out   to go under   from the word go

START AND STOP IDIOMS ● How do you say it?

Get going   Get the show on the road.   Get things moving.   Get cracking.
Get a move on.   Get set.   Get up steam.

Start the ball rolling.   Start off on the right foot.

Set out.   Set off.   Set sail.

Come to a stop / halt / end / close.

Pull up.   Stop dead.   Stop in one's tracks.

Belt up.   Shut up.   Lay off.   Leave off.   Cut it out.   Give it a rest.   Break it up.
Put a sock in it.   Enough is enough.   That's enough.   That will do.

BEGINNERS AND BEGINNINGS

Word bank: source, publication, maiden, origin, outbreak, foundation, inaugurated, opened, established, invented

1 Alexander Graham Bell _____ the telephone in 1876.
2 The _____ of World War 2 was on September 2 1939.
3 Speke identified the _____ of the Nile in 1858.
4 The Titanic sank on her _____ voyage in 1912.
5 A French gardener, Joseph Monier, _____ the technique of reinforcing concrete in 1849 when he needed to make extra large flower pots.
6 *The Old Man of the Sea* was an immediate success from its _____ in 1952.
7 The _____ of Rome is traditionally agreed to have been in BC 509.
8 The Shakespeare Memorial Theatre was _____ at Stratford in 1932.
9 The Olympic Games had their _____ in Greece in BC 776.
10 In 1984 Queen Elizabeth _____ the Thames Barrier which protects London from flooding.

WHAT'S THE DIFFERENCE? ● Translate to show the differences.

Railways Finished.   Railways Closed.   Railway Terminus.

The start of the book.   The introduction of the book.   The launch of the book.
The publication of the book.

Flights delayed.   Flights suspended.   Flights postponed.

Joined the party.   Gate-crashed the party.   Looked in on the party.

Curtail one's holiday.   Interrupt one's holiday.   Delay one's holiday.

TEST YOURSELF ● Listen to the passage being read to you. There are ten spaces in it. In each of the following lists, three of the four words will fit the space (though they may not have exactly the same meaning). You should cross out the unacceptable word. Finally, add your idea of the notion.

				Notion
1 end	closure	shut down	closing down	
2 interrupted	held up	held back	delayed	
3 lull	pause	hold up	gap	
4 opened	started	opened up	inaugurated	
5 leaving	emerging from	coming out of	escaping from	
6 another	a further	an additional	an extra	
7 flee	retire	fly	escape	
8 arrived at	got to	reached	signed in	
9 held up	delayed	interrupted	put back	
10 treat	order	buy	stand	

Unit 19

CUED DIALOGUES
Situation Two neighbours meet.

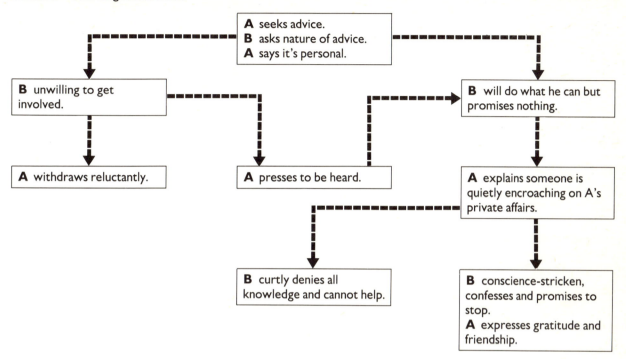

FOR TRANSLATION

a a control column   a control room   a control tower   traffic control
   exchange control   self control   quality control   a controlled experiment
   a controlled skid   under control   out of control   beyond control

b to hold back   a holding company   to hold down   to hold in   to hold off
   to hold one's own   to keep a hold on something   to hold together
   no holds barred   a foothold   a handhold   a toehold   to have a hold over someone
   there's no holding him

c orders   under orders   to give orders   orderly   in good order   order of battle
   the order of the day   sailing orders   marching orders   under sealed orders
   standing orders   a tall order   to keep order   a disorderly house

FINE DISTINCTIONS
● Put + or − in the appropriate boxes to show the elements of meaning in the following verbs. Use your results to make definitions.

	kindness	force	physical	mental	good intentions
influence					
brainwash					
dominate					
persuade					
guide					
imprison					
convince					

● Now translate the verbs into your own language. Use similar labels for the columns, though you may need to change some, or even to add further columns.

IDIOMS ADVISING SELF-CONTROL
● How do you say it?

Keep your hair / shirt on.   Keep your cool.   Stay calm.   Don't lose your cool / temper.
Keep a stiff upper lip.   Keep a straight face.   Keep your chin up.
Keep it under your hat.   Keep it to yourself.   Keep your mouth shut.
Keep your own counsel.   Bite your tongue.
Don't let them get you down.
Count to ten before you lose your temper.

VERBS BECOME NOUNS
● Write the nouns formed from the following verbs in the appropriate columns.

administer   imprison
assert   lead
command   limit
control   manage
detain   navigate
dictate   prohibit
direct   regiment
govern

-ment	-ion	-er
-ship	**-ation**	**-or**

TEST YOURSELF ● Listen to the passage being read to you. There are ten spaces in it. In each of the following lists, three of the four words will fit the space (though they may not have exactly the same meaning). You should cross out the unacceptable word. Finally add your idea of the notion.

				Notion
1 persuaded me	convinced me	made me agree	argued	
2 detected	learned	heard	discovered	
3 a salesman	an agent	a worker	a representative	
4 patterns	segments	examples	samples	
5 pick	choose	elect	select	
6 opinions	hints	suggestions	advice	
7 match	harmonise with	go with	agree with	
8 determine	decide	come to a conclusion about	make our minds up about	
9 inspected	examined	stared at	studied	
10 choice	selection	decision	preference	

Unit 20

CUED DIALOGUES

Situation Interviewer and oldest inhabitant.

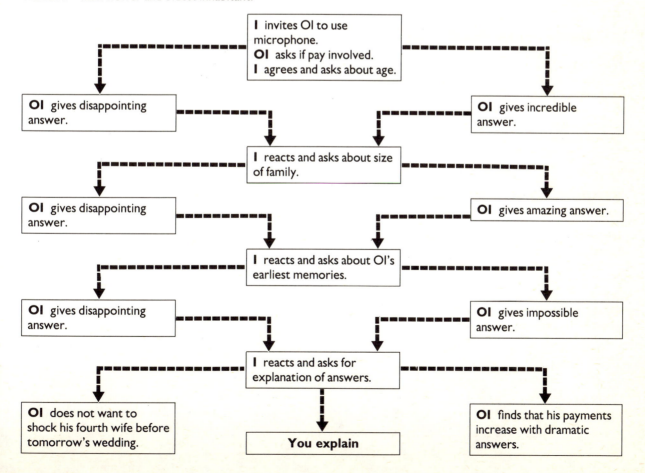

FOR TRANSLATION

a good for nothing   Good Friday   good-humoured   good-looking   good-natured
good-sense   good-tempered   goodwill   to be as good as one's word
for good and all   in one's own good time   in someone's good books   to make good

b badness   bad blood   a bad debt   a bad egg   bad language   a bad shot   to go bad
to go to the bad   in someone's bad books   with a bad grace   in bad faith
to go from bad to worse   to leave a bad taste in one's mouth

WICKED IDIOMS?
● Complete the following idioms and then translate them.

To catch someone ....

To catch someone in the ....

To lie through one's ....

To kill two birds with one ....

To kill the goose that lays the golden ....

To steal someone's ....

To rob Peter to pay ....

To swear like a ....

Crime doesn't ....

SHADES OF MEANING
● Put ticks in the appropriate boxes to show the elements of meaning in each word. Then use your table to write definitions. Experiment below with the parallel set of words in your own language.

	human	animal	plant	legal	in battle
kill					
murder					
execute					
put down					
destroy					
assassinate					
massacre					
slaughter					

PAIN AND PLEASURE ● Arrange the following words from Quentin Crisp's article into two columns, according to whether they have a sense of pain or pleasure. Then put an asterisk (*) against those which are used metaphorically in the article.

admire	loathed
annoyance	impose on
compliment	insulted
enthusiasm	interested
fascinating	massages
fear	nastiness
gifts	nuisance
goaded	placate
gouged	rebuke
harm	soothes
hurt	trying

pain	pleasure

TEST YOURSELF ● Listen to the passage being read to you. There are ten spaces in it. In each of the following lists three of the four words will fit the space (though they may not have exactly the same meaning). You should cross out the unacceptable word. Finally, add your idea of the notion.

				Notion
1 demanded	questioned	asked	inquired	
2 a hostile	an offensive	an unkind	an aggressive	
3 convinced	positive	certain	satisfied	
4 launched	cast	shot	fired	
5 steadily	securely	firmly	doggedly	
6 disturbing	sinister	surprising	alarming	
7 freezing	cool	chilly	nippy	
8 prodded	poked	jabbed	knocked	
9 realigned	straightened	adjusted	shifted	
10 did its job	triumphed	worked	succeeded	

CROSSWORD 1 ● Emotions

Across

- 6 A strong warm feeling (4)
- 7 Make you like someone (6)
- 8 It stands on end when you are afraid (4)
- 9 Become suddenly angry (3,3)
- 10 Love very much (5)
- 11 Quality of attraction and pleasure (5)
- 15 When you have got this you are scared (4,2)
- 18 Furious anger (4)
- 19 Dislike very strongly (6)
- 20 When you are head .... heels in love, you cannot help yourself (4)

Down

- 1 Person who runs away from danger (6)
- 2 Great fear (6)
- 3 Feeling nervous tension (5)
- 4 When you are on .... you are nervous and irritable (4)
- 5 Dislike very strongly (4)
- 12 Another word for 2 (6)
- 13 Feel sorry about (6)
- 14 Emotionally disturbed (5)
- 16 Someone or something you worship (4)
- 17 When you show excessive love for someone, you .... on them (4)

CROSSWORD 2 ● Damage

Across

- 3 Cuts fiercely with a knife (5)
- 6 Mend, put right (6)
- 7 Pierce or stab with a sharp weapon (5)
- 8 When things burn, they burst into ....(6)
- 9 Deliberate damage by fire (5)
- 12 Like a damaged bucket, not water tight (5)
- 15 When ice cream has .... it is ruined (6)
- 16 If you do this in a car you may damage it (5)
- 17 Slightly burned, scorched (6)
- 18 If you injure your hand it may do this, getting bigger (5)

Down

- 1 Makes well again (5)
- 2 Cripples, damages part of the body (5)
- 4 Line or mark made by folding (6)
- 5 Damage clothes by bad washing that makes them get smaller (6)
- 10 Cuts thinly, or thin cuts (6)
- 11 Harm, injury (6)
- 13 If you damage your eyes, you may go .... (5)
- 14 Renovate, restore (5)

CROSSWORD 3 ● Personal qualities

Across

5 Not very good-looking (5)
7 Enjoying (6)
8 Foolishness (5)
9 Powerful, important (6)
12 Sadness (6)
15 Act dishonestly, unfairly (5)
16 Intelligent, bright (6)
17 Opposite of kind (5)

Down

1 Distant, rather unfriendly (5)
2 Foolish (5)
3 Energy, liveliness (6)
4 Intelligent, clever (6)
6 Not beautiful or even plain (4)
10 Ally, person you like (6)
11 Plain-looking (6)
12 Ill, not well (4)
13 Attractive pleasing quality (5)
14 Keen, full of interest (5)

CROSSWORD 4 ● Thought and reason

Across

1 Give information (6)
5 Give a different opinion (5)
6 Choose (6)
8 Intelligence, practical wisdom (5)
9 Idea, concept (6)
15 Foresight, wisdom about the future (6)
16 Discovered (5)
17 Think slowly and carefully (6)
18 Fool, person acting in a silly way (5)
19 Clever, having brains (6)

Down

1 Mad (6)
2 Calculate, determine (6)
3 Belief (5)
4 Form an opinion without careful thought (5)
7 Allows (4)
10 Strength, energy (6)
11 The part of the body that thinks and reasons (4)
12 Vitality, power (6)
13 Foolishness (5)
14 Experienced, held in the mind, familiar (5)

CROSSWORD 5 ● Ups and downs

Across

1. Look down on and laugh at (6)
5. Stand with head and shoulders down (5)
6. Make less (6)
8. Further down (5)
9. Dig underground (6)
15. Dive (6)
16. Raised, made bigger (5)
17. Fall in a clumsy way (6)
18. Let fall or run down (5)
19. Going up, a climb (6)

Down

1. Water down, make weaker (6)
2. Make deeper (6)
3. Opposite of sat down (5)
4. With head bent down, in respect (5)
7. Go down in water (4)
10. When your head's up in them you're happy (6)
11. A ………. nose is turned up (4)
12. Bring down, beat, overcome (6)
13. Falls or lets fall (5)
14. Become big, like wet wood (5)

CROSSWORD 6 ● Strength and weakness

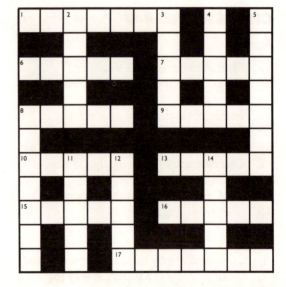

Across

1. Tiredness (7)
6. Power, strength (5)
7. Weaken by slowly wearing away (5)
8. Full of life, lively (5)
9. Tightly stretched, under strain (5)
10. All the ……… in a chain must be strong (5)
13. Powerful explosion (5)
15. Foreign (5)
16. Physically weak, losing consciousness (5)
17. Makes weak (7)

Down

2. Fastened strongly, not slack or loose (5)
3. You ……… all your strength when you try your hardest (5)
4. A king wears it on his head as a sign of his power (5)
5. Most eager (7)
8. Measurement of electro-motive force (7)
11. As hard as ……… (5)
12. Strong cord that joins muscles to bones (5)
14. Opposite of dead (5)

CROSSWORD 7 ● On foot

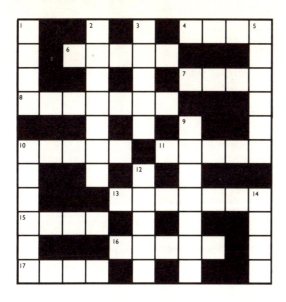

Across

4 Jump lightly from one foot to the other (4)
6 You take them as you walk (5)
7 Walk slowly and heavily (4)
8 Walk in a self-satisfied way (7)
10 Move on hands and knees (5)
11 Walk sideways, shyly (5)
13 Ran with quick, light steps (7)
15 Each foot has five (4)
16 Remain upright (5)
17 Go quickly (4)

Down

1 Goes on foot quickly (4)
2 Walk in a drunken, unsteady way (7)
3 Pace (5)
5 Walk in shallow water (6)
9 Walking lamely (7)
10 (of horses) An easy gallop (6)
12 Runs slowly (5)
14 Rush (4)

CROSSWORD 8 ● Communication

Across

5 Produce a book or newspaper (5)
7 Paper pinned on a board to give information (6)
8 Speak (5)
9 Tell someone what something is worth (6)
12 Warning of an intention to hurt or punish (6)
15 Beg, request very seriously (5)
16 Written communication (6)
17 Deaf and dumb people communicate by these (5)

Down

1 Communicate by making marks on paper (5)
2 Speak proudly in a superior way (5)
3 Grumble (6)
4 Sent by mail, posted (6)
6 Latest information, as carried by newspapers (4)
10 Author, producer of letters (6)
11 Documents (6)
12 Narrate, inform (4)
13 Allege, declare (5)
14 Curses, sends to eternal punishment (5)

CROSSWORD 9 ● Opinion

Across

3 Regard, consider (4)
6 Have faith, believe in (5)
7 It's my .... means it's my opinion (6)
9 Draw meaning or opinion from something (5)
10 Understand from something said (6)
14 Calculate (6)
17 Our opinions are held in our .... (5)
18 Logical, reasoned opinion, sometimes unproved (6)
19 Scientific, formal reasoning (5)
20 Assume means .... for granted (4)

Down

1 Concede, allow (5)
2 Requested an opinion (5)
4 .... up means tries to form an opinion (6)
5 Give an opinion to someone (6)
8 Your opinions must be sound when you are doing an .... (4)
11 One who gives an opinion, often finding fault (6)
12 Take, believe an opinion (6)
13 You have a .... opinion of those you despise (4)
15 One who stubbornly holds an opinion (5)
16 You change your opinion when you .... you were wrong (5)

CROSSWORD 10 ● Rise and Fall

Across

1 Make smaller (6)
6 Having got big (5)
7 Grows quickly (6)
8 Gets larger (5)
12 He climbs up and down (11)
13 Cuts down with an axe (5)
17 Higher (6)
18 Reduces to a liquid (5)
19 Inflate (4,2)

Down

1 Get up—like the sun (4)
2 Fall (4)
3 Reductions (4)
4 Getting bigger (7)
5 Larger than normal (7)
9 Let down, sent down (7)
10 Fill with air (7)
11 Hang down heavily (3)
14 Drop down (4)
15 Rising of the tide: opposite of ebb (4)
16 Fall in small drops (4)

CROSSWORD 11 ● In the future

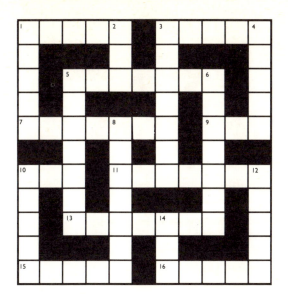

Across

1. Astrologers read your future in your .... (5)
3. If you have no appointments tomorrow, it's a .... day (5)
5. He .... into my shoes = He replaced me (7)
7. Person who makes prophecies (7)
9. What we do to seeds to ensure a future crop (3)
10. I'll eat my .... = I don't believe something (3)
11. Person who tells the future by reading your hand (7)
13. Person who takes shelter from approaching danger (7)
15. Physical exercise, practice (5)
16. Someone anxious to improve in the future .... over a new leaf (5)

Down

1. When you put off a difficult decision, you may decide to .... on it (5)
2. Parents often side-step children's questions by saying 'Wait and ....' (3)
3. Money saved up for future use (7)
4. Put new life into, restore (5)
5. Light motorcycle (7)
6. Decide in advance: He was ....d to be a soldier (7)
8. Optimistic about the future (7)
10. Carefully save and store up valuable things (5)
12. .... the consequences = accepts what follows as a result (5)
14. .... ready = prepare (3)

CROSSWORD 12 ● Change

Across

7. As time passes we all get this (5)
8. Make changes (5)
9. Join one thing to another (3)
10. Mature person (5)
11. Chews and swallows (4)
12. We're not as young as we .... to be (4)
19. Wear down (5)
20. Decay (3)
21. Reduces to a useless state (5)
22. Release, free (5)

Down

1. Travel by ship (6)
2. Change, modify, rearrange according to need (6)
3. Rub into small pieces against a rough surface (5)
4. Lost colour (5)
5. Put a halt to (4)
6. Make neat by cutting pieces off (4)
13. Remove creases or obstacles (6)
14. Make deeper (6)

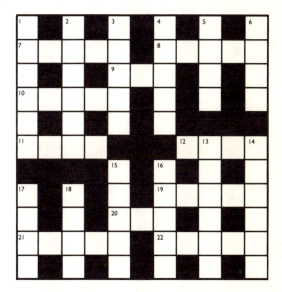

15. Deteriorate = get .... (5)
16. Leave one's bed, rise (3,2)
17. Change, make different (4)
18. Wound or injure (4)

CROSSWORD 13 ● Impact

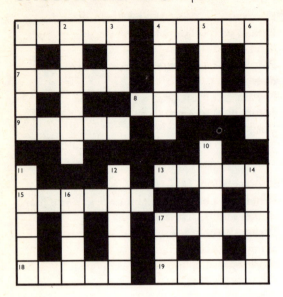

Across
1. Strike with the fist (5)
4. You dig someone in the ribs with it (5)
7. Bend by turning (5)
8. White sheet on which films are projected (6)
9. Dig these in if you are stubborn (5)
13. What tyres do when punctured (5)
15. Collision, two objects striking (6)
17. Cut a thin piece (5)
18. Burn slightly, scorch (5)
19. Sheds tears (5)

Down
1. Throw (5)
2. Clashes and clangs are .... of impact (6)
3. Strike (3)
4. Throw out (5)
5. Mark or cut up with the teeth (4)
6. Hurt, harm (5)
10. Discoloured flesh after a blow (6)
11. Impacts from the foot (5)
12. Cut or scratch with a sharp point (5)
14. Travels, makes a long journey (5)
16. What you feel after an impact (4)
17. A wood-cutting tool with teeth (3)

CROSSWORD 14 ● Together and apart

Across
1. Cuts into pieces (5)
3. Collected money (5)
5. One who learns (7)
7. Gathered together in bunches (7)
9. Soil and water mixed together (3)
10. Long narrow strip of wood for moving over snow (3)
11. Taking away or leaving a house (7)
13. Put together in groups (7)
15. Wed, join as husband and wife (5)
16. Group of people with one origin, language and customs living together as a community (5)

Down
1. Smallest piece of bread or cake (5)
2. Large body of salt water (3)
3. United country under a king (7)
4. Joined by a yoke (5)
5. Joining together like a chain (7)
6. Taken away (7)
8. Notes sounding well together (7)
10. Many bees together (5)
12. Go away from (5)

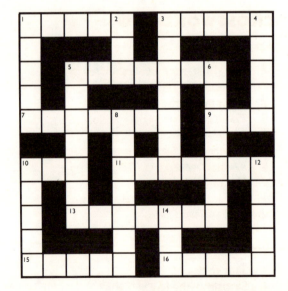

14. .... your heads together — think about something together (3)

CROSSWORD 15 ● Relationships

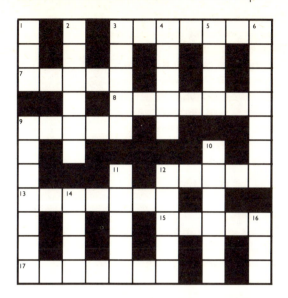

Across

3 From one end or side to another (7)
7 Look after the sick (5)
8 Near to and opposing (7)
9 Childless couples sometimes .... children (5)
12 Over, higher than (5)
13 If you are ...., someone is following (7)
15 Voters do it to a successful candidate (5)
17 Disagree with (7)

Down

1 Blood relations (3)
2 Take from a lender (6)
3 Doctors do it to patients (5)
4 Competitor (5)
5 On the surface of (4)
6 Unfriendly, aggressive (7)
9 What candidates did for their jobs (7)
10 People or things for others to copy (6)
11 Brother's daughter (5)
12 One who acts for you (5)
14 Copies like a monkey (4)
16 Join with a knot (3)

CROSSWORD 16 ● Start and finish

Across

3 Cut short, stop something early (7)
7 The same again (5)
8 Begins a journey, leaves (4,3)
9 To .... in, is to enter rudely (5)
12 Sunset is the .... the day (3,2)
14 Become less loud, hot or violent (3, 4)
15 Animals' end parts (5)
17 Escape (3,4)

Down

1 Beginning of a flower (3)
2 Go into (5)
3 Shut (5)
4 Stops moving (5)
5 What moving things finally come to (1,4)
6 Start for a rocket (4,3)
9 Beginning to develop (7)
10 First appearance in public (5)
11 To put seed in the ground (2,3)
12 Place where you go in (5)
13 Finishing one's life (5)
16 Go down like the sun (3)

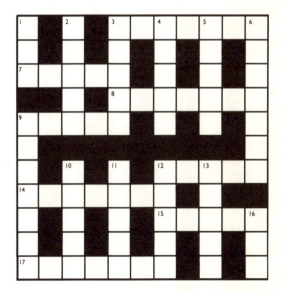

CROSSWORD 17 ● Control

Across

- 3 Track—control and check, e.g. a rocket (7)
- 7 Put pressure on (5)
- 8 One who offers temptation (7)
- 9 Law breaking which the police control (5)
- 12 Opposite of closes (5)
- 13 He runs a business (7)
- 16 Collections of laws, systems of rules (5)
- 18 Takes weapons from (7)

Down

- 1 Short for representative (3)
- 2 Detain (4,2)
- 3 Get on top of, control (6)
- 4 What is usual, a standard of proper behaviour (4)
- 5 Skill and understanding needed to control people (4)
- 6 Keep down, keep under, control (7)
- 9 Be in charge of (7)
- 10 Compels (6)
- 11 He is in front or in charge (6)
- 14 Awaited information (4)
- 15 A .... lever is part of a car's controls (4)
- 17 .... to = take care of, attend to (3)

CROSSWORD 18 ● Vice and virtue

Across

- 3 It goes with **smash** (4)
- 6 Dishonest trickery, usually for money (5)
- 7 Terrorists spread it (6)
- 9 You are in the wrong when you are at this (5)
- 10 Wicked (6)
- 14 What a foul-mouthed person does (6)
- 17 Serious lawbreaking (5)
- 18 Morally bad, corrupt (6)
- 19 Put to bad use, treat roughly or cruelly (5)
- 20 Strong jealousy (4)

Down

- 1 What villains do to the law (5)
- 2 The fact of having done wrong (5)
- 4 Robbed, made sad and hopeless (6)
- 5 Standards of behaviour; good principles (6)
- 8 Wickedness (4)
- 11 To corrupt people is to lead them .... (6)
- 12 Kind, mild, not rough (6)
- 13 Loyal, faithful (4)
- 15 Money wrongly offered (5)
- 16 It goes with **grab** (5)

Some English idioms

all ears listening with full attention *He was all ears when he heard his name mentioned.*
all the best good luck *All the best for your new job.*
as good as one's word true to one's promises *He said he would help and he was as good as his word.*
at a loose end having nothing to do *I'm at a loose end this morning.*
at short notice with little warning *She took the job at short notice.*
at sixes and sevens in confusion *The office was at sixes and sevens.*
at the drop of a hat immediately *If you invite her she'll come at the drop of a hat.*
back to square one back to the original situation *We lost everything in the fire: it was back to square one.*
bad blood bad feelings *There's bad blood between their families.*
bad egg bad person *Don't trust him, he's a bad egg.*
(in) bad faith dishonestly *I've discovered that the dealer was acting in bad faith.*
(with) bad grace impolitely *He took the court's decision with bad grace, shouting at the judge.*
bad taste in one's mouth disgust *Their insulting behaviour left us all with a bad taste in our mouths.*
ball of fire very lively person *He'll make the party a success; he's a real ball of fire.*
beat about the bush not say directly what one means *Why beat about the bush, if you've nothing to hide?*
behind the scenes not in public view *He would not have won the election without many supporters working behind the scenes.*
below the belt unfair *That remark was below the belt.*
belt up (*informal*) be quiet *Finally I just told him to belt up.*
birds of a feather (flock together) people with similar interests *You rarely meet them apart, they're such birds of a feather.*
bite one's tongue stop oneself from speaking *I had to bite my tongue to avoid giving offence.*
break one's heart make one suffer deeply *It will break his heart if she dies.*
break the ice make a friendly start *To break the ice he told one of his amusing stories.*
break the news tell someone (usually bad) news *Who will break the news of the accident to her?*
bring someone down to earth make them accept reality *Having to take a job brought him down to earth.*
bring to light discover *The theft was brought to light by chance.*
by all means certainly *'May I come in?' 'By all means.'*
by leaps and bounds very quickly, greatly *She's improving by leaps and bounds.*
by the skin of one's teeth narrowly *She passed the examination by the skin of her teeth.*
call a spade a spade speak frankly and openly *You know exactly where you are with him; he always calls a spade a spade.*
can't help can't avoid or stop *I couldn't help laughing when I saw them.*
can't teach an old dog new tricks older people do not easily change their ways *A computer is no use to him – you can't teach an old dog new tricks.*
cat in hell's chance no chance at all *Why is he trying to become a lawyer? He hasn't a cat in hell's chance.*
catch one's eye be noticed *It caught my eye so I bought it.*
catch in the act find someone doing wrong *The thieves were caught in the act.*
change one's tune act differently *You'll change your tune after you have had children.*
child's play very easy *Learning to type is child's play.*
cold feet state of fear *I've got cold feet about the exam.*
come down on someone like a ton of bricks punish, be angry with someone *If I'm late, he comes down on me like a ton of bricks.*
come in handy be useful *Take an umbrella; it might come in handy.*
come to the point get to the important part of what one is saying *To my surprise, he came to the point at once.*
count one's chickens before they are hatched rely on the results before they appear *It's not certain you will be left anything in the will, so don't count your chickens before they are hatched.*
cross one's fingers hope for good luck *My*

interview is on Monday so keep your fingers crossed for me.
cut it out (*informal*)   stop it   *He was being rude, so I told him to cut it out.*
dog's life   unhappy existence   *Their brother was a bully and led them a dog's life.*
draw the line (at)   decide that one has had enough of something   *Mother let us keep pets, but she drew the line at a lion cub.*
drop a hint   give a suggestion   *He dropped me a hint it would be advisable to stay away from the meeting.*
drop (someone) a line   send a short letter   *Drop me a line when you get back home.*
ears burn   feel embarrassed because people are talking about you   *My ears were burning during their meeting.*
every so often   occasionally   *He only inspected the books every so often.*
eyes in the back of one's head   ability to know everything that is happening   *With those children, you need eyes in the back of your head.*
fall head over heels (in love)   fall deeply in love   *The moment he saw her he fell head over heels.*
fifty-fifty   evenly both ways   *They shared the costs fifty-fifty.*
finger in the pie   involvement in something   *He's a very active politician; he's got a finger in every pie.*
first come, first served   first arrivals get first attention   *Don't push in; we work on the principle of first come, first served.*
fish out of water   someone uncomfortable because of a strange situation   *At the ladies' club he felt like a fish out of water.*
follow in someone's footsteps   do the same as someone before   *She's following in her father's footsteps and becoming a doctor.*
for the time being   meanwhile   *Dinner will be ready in an hour; have a biscuit for the time being.*
free agent   one who can do what he/she likes   *Stay out as late as you like; after all, you're a free agent.*
free and easy   not formal   *The atmosphere in the hotel was free and easy.*
from bad to worse   deteriorating   *After his illness, his work went from bad to worse.*
get a move on   hurry up   *Get a move on or you'll be late.*
get cracking (*informal*)   start doing something at once   *Let's get cracking; there's a lot to be done.*
get going   start moving   *It's a long way, so let's get going.*
get off on the wrong foot   begin badly   *We got off on the wrong foot when he said his father hated mine.*
get one's own back   have one's revenge   *You've won today, but next time we play I'll get my own back.*
get the show on the road   make arrangements work   *She called a planning meeting to get the show on the road at once.*
get things moving   make things work   *Without any equipment we'll never get things moving.*
get up steam   prepare to act   *We're getting up steam for the election.*
give a hand   help, assist   *Can you give me a hand with this case?*
give the game away   tell a secret   *This is a surprise present for her, so please don't give the game away like last time.*
give someone a piece of one's mind   speak frankly, often complaining, to someone   *When she sees him she's going to give him a piece of her mind.*
go like clockwork   go smoothly   *It was well planned so it went like clockwork.*
go one's own way   do as one wishes   *He always goes his own way, so don't waste time with your advice.*
go to the dogs   deteriorate, get worse   *There's no discipline any more; this school is going to the dogs.*
have a go   try   *I've never played before, but I'll have a go.*
have bats in the belfry   be a bit eccentric, mad   *She had bats in the belfry. She couldn't talk to anyone without reciting Shakespeare at them.*
have one's hands full   be very busy   *Her assistant was ill so she had her hands full.*
have one's hands tied   be prevented from acting   *The law says he must not sell you cigarettes; so even if he wants to, his hands are tied.*
have one's heart in one's mouth   be afraid   *As she crossed the narrow bridge she had her heart in her mouth.*
have the best of both worlds   enjoy the advantages of both situations   *Her mother looks after the baby, so she can keep her job and have the best of both worlds.*
have words   quarrel   *Don't go in there; they're having words.*
high and dry   alone and helpless   *When father died I was left high and dry.*
hit the nail on the head   say something that is exactly correct   *Her criticism hit the nail on the head.*
hold one's tongue   be silent   *You were wise to hold your tongue.*
hot air   meaningless talk   *His advice is just a lot of hot air.*
in a cold sweat   in great fear   *On take-off I was in a cold sweat.*
in a nut-shell   briefly   *What, in a nut-shell, is your objection?*
in someone's bad books   disliked by someone   *She'll never get promotion, she's in the boss's bad books.*

in stitches laughing a lot *His stories had us all in stitches.*
in the dark uninformed *They kept us in the dark about their intentions.*
in the same boat in the same situation *You won't be allowed to have special treatment because we're all in the same boat.*
keep an eye on watch, guard *Keep an eye on the baby please.*
keep one's chin up stay cheerful *Try to keep your chin up; the situation can't go on for ever.*
keep one's cool (*informal*) not panic *The dog won't attack if we keep our cool.*
keep one's hair on (*informal*) not get angry *No one's insulted you; keep your hair on.*
keep one's mouth shut remain silent *Having heard their threats, he kept his mouth firmly shut.*
keep something under one's hat keep something secret *I think there might be a wedding, but keep it under your hat.*
kill two birds with one stone achieve two aims by one action *While you're taking the dog for a walk, call in at the shop for me and kill two birds with one stone.*
lead a dog's life be unhappy *With so little money, they lead a dog's life.*
lead someone a dance avoid being caught *The thief led the police a dance for several months before he was caught.*
lead someone by the nose make someone do as you want *His friend is a bad influence; she leads him by the nose.*
lead someone up the garden path deceive someone *He led us up the garden path by claiming to be an inspector.*
leopard never changes its spots people don't change their nature *You'll never make her work hard; a leopard never changes its spots.*
let off steam express strong feelings *After the exam they had a party to let off steam.*
let the cat out of the bag reveal a secret *If you let the cat out the bag I'll never tell you another secret.*
look before you leap think before action *In choosing a husband it is wise to look before you leap.*
lose one's grip become less efficient *Now she's getting old she's beginning to lose her grip on the business.*
lose one's nerve become afraid *When he saw the height of the mountain, he lost his nerve and turned back.*
lose one's temper become angry *She was a good teacher and never lost her temper.*
make a mountain out of a mole-hill make something sound bigger or worse than it is *The child cried at every little scratch; he always made mountains out of mole-hills.*
make fun of laugh at *The boys made fun of their teacher.*

make one's mouth water fill one with anticipation *The wonderful dresses in the Paris shops would make her mouth water.*
man in the street ordinary person *To the man in the street, football is more interesting than politics.*
meet one's eye come to one's attention *Landing in England, the first thing to meet the eye is the greenery.*
meet someone halfway compromise *The government met the strikers' demands halfway.*
mind one's own business not interfere with other people's affairs *Why can't your mother mind her own business?*
never mind don't worry (about) *I've lost my pen, but never mind, I can borrow yours.*
nip something in the bud stop something before it develops *This unrest must be nipped in the bud before there's a riot.*
old hand experienced person *Get Tom to look at your car; he's an old hand with engines.*
on cloud nine (*informal*) extremely happy *When they're together, they both appear to be on cloud nine.*
on edge tense *She felt on edge while waiting for the doctor.*
on the tip of one's tongue almost remembered but not quite *His name's on the tip of my tongue, but I just can't recall it.*
out of order not working *The heating's out of order and I'm cold.*
pick someone's brains get information from someone *Can I pick your brains about the best places for my shopping?*
play safe take not risks *The car's not reliable; we'll play safe and take a taxi.*
play the game do something fairly *You shouldn't do his homework for him; it's not playing the game.*
play with fire act dangerously *Anyone experimenting with drugs is playing with fire.*
pull oneself together regain control of oneself *Although she had not slept, she pulled herself together and went to work.*
pull one's weight do one's share of work *There's a lot to do so everyone must pull their weight.*
pull someone's leg play a joke on someone *When they said his house was on fire they were only pulling his leg.*
put a sock in it (*informal*) stop it *You're always complaining; I wish you'd put a sock in it.*
put one's foot down insist on something *Since father put his foot down about watching television, he's done his homework.*
put one's house in order arrange one's affairs *The old woman put her house in order by making a will a year before she died.*
put one's shoulder to the wheel help to get

something done *If we are to raise the money, everyone must put their shoulders to the wheel.*

put someone's nose out of joint offend/embarrass someone *Apparently I put his nose out of joint by applying for the job.*

put two and two together come to an obvious conclusion *His shoes were wet, so, putting two and two together, I decided he had been outside.*

put your heads together share your ideas *Their parents put their heads together to decide on a family holiday.*

rain cats and dogs rain heavily *I'm staying in; it's raining cats and dogs outside.*

read between the lines see an unstated meaning *I've just heard from mother, and reading between the lines, she's not very well.*

rock the boat act independently and cause problems to colleagues *If anyone talks to the press at this time it could rock the boat.*

rule the roost take command *The deputy chairman seems to rule the roost in this committee.*

rule with a rod of iron keep very strict control *Those boys soon get out of hand unless they are ruled with a rod of iron.*

see the light change one's views for better ones *Fortunately she saw the light six months before the exam and started to work.*

set someone's mind at rest stop them worrying *The news of his safe arrival set her mind at rest.*

set the table prepare a table for a meal *Before you set the table, just wipe it over, please.*

sit on the fence not take sides *The ministers argued for hours while the Prime Minister sat on the fence.*

snake in the grass person who cannot be trusted *After all the secrets she has told him, he has proved to be a snake in the grass.*

spin a yarn tell amusingly untrue stories *People don't take him seriously because he spins such yarns.*

split one's sides laugh greatly *They watched an old silent film and split their sides with laughing.*

split the difference make a bargain by agreeing on the halfway point between the two offers *Let's split the difference.*

stand on one's own feet be independent *She refused to support the boy any longer, saying that he must learn to stand on his own two feet.*

start the ball rolling begin something for others to continue *They seemed shy so I started the ball rolling by telling a few stories.*

step into someone's shoes replace someone in an expected way *When the chairman retired, his daughter stepped into his shoes.*

stiff upper lip ability to hide one's feelings *If our leaders don't keep a stiff upper lip, we shall become down-hearted when they do.*

strike while the iron is hot act when the time is suitable *Seeing his father in a good mood, the boy struck while the iron was hot and asked for more pocket money.*

take a back seat be less important than before *Once she lost the support of her colleagues she had to take a back seat.*

take a hint recognise a hidden message *When I looked at my watch, they took the hint and left.*

take it easy relax *She needs to take it easy for a while.*

take place happen *The story of the novel took place in Russia.*

take someone's breath away amaze someone *The news of winning all that money took her breath away.*

take steps take a course of action *After the flood, steps are being taken to ensure it never happens again.*

take the bull by the horns tackle the problem firmly and fearlessly *I didn't want to complain, but I was so angry that I eventually took the bull by the horns, and spoke out.*

take to one's heels run away *The thief took to his heels.*

talk shop talk about one's job *She's a bore, always talking shop.*

through and through completely *She's an angel, through and through.*

thumb a lift beg a ride by a thumb gesture *When the car broke down I thumbed a lift to the nearest garage.*

tie (someone) in knots confuse (someone) *She's so clever; she ties everybody in knots with her arguments.*

tied to one's mother's apron-strings totally under one's mother's influence *He may be 30 but he's till tied to his mother's apron-strings.*

have time on one's hands have time to spare *He would get into less mischief if he had less time on his hands.*

turn over a new leaf deliberately improve one's behaviour *This folly has to stop; it's time you turned over a new leaf.*

turn the tables change the fortunes of a contest for the better *He threw back the grenade before it exploded and so turned the tables on the enemy.*

twist someone's arm persuade someone to do something *Well, if you twist my arm, I suppose there's time for another drink.*

under someone's thumb under someone's control *She has her whole family under her thumb.*

under the weather slightly unwell *She's felt under the weather for two or three months now.*

water off a duck's back something that has no effect *They warned him often, but it was water off a duck's back.*
when in Rome (do as the Romans do) in foreign countries or strange places, behave as they do *Although it was well past my usual bed-time, I went out with my host – when in Rome...*
you don't say expression of surprise *'He's been invited to the Palace.' 'You don't say!'*

Note: For obvious reasons, this list is highly selective. For more idioms, see M.J. Wallace, *Dictionary of English Idioms*, Collins 1981.

Echo phrases

again and again	enough is enough	man to man	shoulder to shoulder
arm in arm	eye to eye	mile after mile	side by side
back to back	face to face	on and on	so and so
bit by bit	fair is fair	one by one	step by step
by and by	hand over hand	out and out	such and such
day after day	hand to hand	over and over	through and through
day by day	heart to heart	more and more	time after time
day to day	house to house	round and round	word for word
door to door	little by little		

Irreversible phrases

back to front	give and take	man and wife	thick and thin
bed and breakfast	great and small	more or less	this and that
bread and butter	head to foot	now and then	to and fro
come and go	here and there	rise and fall	top to toe
cup and saucer	high and low	start to finish	up and down
fish and chips	hither and thither	stop and start	ups and downs
flesh and blood	in and out		

Some English similes

as black as thunder
as blind as a bat
as bold as brass
as brown as a berry
as busy as a bee
as clean as a new pin
as clean as a whistle
as clear as a bell
as clear as mud*
as cold as ice
as cool as a cucumber
as cunning as a fox
as dead as a doornail
as dry as a bone
as dull as ditchwater
as easy as ABC
as fat as a pig
as fat as butter
as fit as a fiddle
as flat as a pancake
as fresh as a daisy
as gentle as a lamb
as good as gold
as green as grass
as happy as a lark

as happy as a sandboy
as hard as nails
as hungry as a hunter
as large as life
as light as a feather
as like as two peas
as mad as a hatter
as mad as a March hare
as nutty as a fruitcake
as obstinate as a mule
as old as the hills
as playful as a kitten
as playful as a puppy
as pleased as Punch
as poor as a church
   mouse
as pretty as a picture
as quick as lightning
as quiet as a mouse
as red as a beetroot
as regular as clockwork
as right as rain
as safe as houses
as sharp as a needle
as sharp as a razor

as sick as a dog
as silent as the grave
as slow as a snail
as slow as a tortoise
as sober as a judge
as soft as butter
as sound as a bell
as steady as a rock
as straight as an arrow
as strong as an ox
as thick as thieves
as thick as two short
   planks
as thin as a rake
as white as a ghost
as white as a sheet
as white as snow

like a bat out of hell
like a bear with a sore
   head
like a cat on hot bricks
like a dog with two tails
like a duck to water
like a fish out of water

like a hole in the head
like a hot potato
like a red rag to a bull
like a shot
like a sore thumb
like birds of a feather
like lambs to the
   slaughter
like water off a ducks
   back

cry like a baby
drink like a fish
eat like pig
feel like a million dollars
fit like a glove
run like the wind
sell like hot cakes
sink like a stone
sleep like a top
spend money like water
spread like wild fire
swear like a trooper
swim like a fish
tremble like a leaf

*Means totally unclear!

Functions

A INTERACTION

A1 Attracting attention
(*polite*) Hello. I say … Excuse me …
Excuse me please, but …
Sorry to trouble you, but …
(*impolite*) Hey. Hi, you … You there…
Look here …

A2 Saying hello
Hi. (*v. informal*) Hi there. (*US informal*)
Hello. Hello, how are you?
How do you do?
Good morning/afternoon/evening.

A3 Introducing oneself
I'm Clive. My name's Clive.
I'm called Clive.
(*on the telephone*) This is Clive. It's Clive.
It's Clive here. Clive here.

A4 Introducing someone else
(*informal*) Clive, this is Carol.
Clive, meet Carol. Have you met Carol?
(*formal*) I'd like you to meet Carol.
I want you to meet Carol.
I don't think you've met Carol.
Let me introduce you to Carol.
I'd like to introduce you to Carol.
May I introduce you to Carol?
Allow me to introduce you. Clive, this is Carol. Carol, this is Clive.

A5 Replying to introductions
(*informal*) Good to see you.
Good to know you.
Pleased to meet you. (*uneducated*)
(*formal*) Delighted to meet you.
How nice to meet you.
The pleasure's mine.
It's nice to meet you.
It's a pleasure to meet you. How nice.
Delighted. I've heard about you.
I've heard a lot about you.
I've been looking forward to meeting you.

A6 Breaking off
I'm going now. I'll be going. I'll be off.
I'll have to be off. I'm on my way.
I'll be getting along.
I must be getting along.
(*informal*) Sorry, but I must dash.
Sorry, but I must fly.
I'm afraid I'll have to be going/leaving/moving.
(*politely informal*) Perhaps you will excuse me, but …
Please don't think I'm rude, but …

A7 Saying goodbye
(*informal*) 'Bye. 'Bye now. 'Bye for now.
See you. See you soon.
Bye-bye. (*casual, also childish*)
So long. (*US informal*)
Ta-ta. (*uneducated, also childish*) Goodbye.
Cheerio. Cheers.

A8 Good wishes at parting
Have a good day/night/weekend/time/holiday/flight/trip/journey. Safe journey.
Happy landing. Drive carefully.
Take care.
Come back safely/all in one piece.
All the best. Have fun. Enjoy yourself.
Be good.

A9 Keeping someone talking
(*showing understanding*) Yes. I see.
Go on. Yes, go on. Yes, I understand.
Yes, I'm with you. Yes, I follow.
And then –?
(*showing interest/disbelief*) You don't say!
Well now! Would you believe it! Amazing!
Well I never! (*informal*)

A10 Making requests
(*spoken*) May I have the salt, please?
Pass the salt, please. Please pass the salt.
I'd like the salt please.
Would you pass the salt, please?
Would you mind passing the salt, please?
Pass the salt, would you?
Let me have the salt, will you?
Would you like to pass the salt?
Do you think I might have the salt
(*written*) You are requested to be punctual.

---

* In this section the different ways of stating the same idea do not necessarily have the same value.

Punctuality is requested.
Patients are requested to be punctual.
Would patients kindly be punctual.
It would be appreciated if patients could be punctual.
It is requested that patients are punctual.
Patients should be punctual.

A11 Saying thank you
(*informal*)   Thanks.   Thanks very much.
Thanks a lot.   Many thanks.   Thank you.
Thank you very much.
Thank you very much indeed.
(*warm*)   You're very kind.   That's very kind.
That's very kind of you.   How kind.
(*formal*)   I'm most grateful.
I'm most grateful. Please accept my thanks.
You've been very helpful.
(*uneducated, also childish*)   Ta.

A12 Replying to thanks (spoken)
(*informal*)   That's OK.   It's OK.   Forget it.
(*formal*)   Not at all.   That's all right.
You're welcome.   Don't mention it.
It's a pleasure.   It's nothing, really.
It's no trouble.

A13 Saying No, thank you
No, thanks.   No, thanks very much.
That's very kind, but no thanks.
I'd rather not.   I think I'd better not.
Perhaps you'd excuse me, this time.
I'll give it a miss this time, if you don't mind.
Perhaps next time.
Count me out, if you don't mind.
Not for me, if you don't mind.
(*refusing drink or food*)   No more, thanks.
I've had quite sufficient, thank you.
Thanks, but I've done very well/
I've had more than enough.
Sorry, but I'm going to have to refuse.
I'd rather not, thank you.

B INFORMATION

B1 Asking for information (general)
(*directly*)   Can you tell/show me ...
Would you explain/advise/inform me ...
Can you help me to find out ...
Would you mind telling/showing/explaining etc. ...
(*indirectly*)   I'd like/love to know ...
I need to find out/to know ...
I want to know ...
I'm afraid I don't know/understand/remember ...

I'm wondering/trying to find out/trying to discover ...
I seem to have forgotten ...
I wish I knew ...   If only I knew ...

B2 Asking about someone's health
(*informal*)   How's Peter?
How's he getting on?   How's he doing?
(*neutral*)   Can you tell me how Peter is?
I'd like to know how Peter is.
(*formal*)   I'm inquiring about Peter Smith.

B3 Asking for details
(*size*)   Is it big?   How big/small is it?
What's the size of the hall?
What's the size like?
Is there much space for ... ?
(*contents*)   Is there a garage?
Has it got a garage?   What about a garage?
Does it have a garage?
How many rooms are there?   What's it got?
(*age*)   How old is it?   Is it old or new?
What's its age?   How long has it been there?
(*location*)   Where's the bathroom?
Is the bathroom up here?
I don't see the bathroom.
How do I find the bathroom?
Can you show me the bathroom?
(*price*)   How much is it?   What's the price?
What does it cost?
What are you asking for it?
(*direction*)   Where's the station?
Where's the station, please?
Which way's the station, please?
Which way to the station, please?
Can you direct me to the station, please?
Can you show me the way to the station, please?
Can you show me how to get to the station, please?
Would you mind showing me to the station, please?
I'm looking for the station – can you help me?

B4 Identifying things
This one.   That one.   The big one.
The other one.   The table near the door.
That table that's near the door.
The table which is near the door.
The house with the blue door.
The house that's painted blue.
The blue-painted house.   The blue house.

B5 Identifying people
Him.   Her.   Them.   Those two.
The girl in green.   The girl wearing green.
The girl who's wearing green.

The man in front of her.
The man standing in front of her.
The man who's standing in front of her.
The girl I saw.   The girl that I saw.

B6   Asking for personal details

official	neutral	informal
Name, please?	What's your name/What are you called?	What do they call you?
Address, please?	What's your address?/Where do you live?	
Date of birth?	What's your date of birth/When were you born?	
Age please?	What's your age?/How old are you?	
Place of birth?	Where were you born?	
Nationality, please?	What's your nationality? What country are you from?	Where are you from?
Occupation, please?	What's your occupation/job?	What do you do?

B7   Talking about someone's appearance

(*height*)   He's tall.
He's lanky. (*uncomplimentary*)
He's of medium/average height.
He's neither tall nor short.
He's short/small/not very tall.
He's on the short side/rather short.
He's tiny.
(*build*)   He's fat/overweight. (*impolite*)
He's stout/heavy. (*polite*)
He's broad/stocky/well-built/thick-set.
He's of average/medium build.
He's neither fat not thin.
He's got a good figure.
He's thin/slight/slim.
He's skinny. (*impolite*)
He's lean. (*of men only*)
She's slender. (*of women only*)
(*hair*)   Her hair's dark.   She's got dark hair.
She's dark-haired.
Her hair's long and wavy.
She's got long, wavy hair.
His hair's fine/coarse/wiry/bushy.
He's going bald.   He's got a bald head.
He's bald-headed.   His hair's rather thin.
He's getting thin on top.
He's got a moustache/beard/sideboards.
He's clean-shaven.
(*skin*)   She's fair/dark.
She's fair-skinned/dark-skinned.
Her complexion is fair/dark.
She's got a fair/dark complexion.
She's tanned.   She's got a tan.
(*age*)   She's young.   She's quite young.
She's youngish.   She looks young.
She's fairly young.
She's in her teens/twenties/thirties/forties/fifties etc.
She is in her early twenties/mid-twenties/late twenties.   She's middle-aged.
She's getting on.   She carries her age well.
She looks young for her age.
She wears well. (*informal*)   She's elderly.
She's very old.   She's ancient. (*impolite*)
(*looks*) – *of women* –   pretty/attractive/lovely/beautiful/plain/homely
She's very pretty.   She's an attractive girl.
– *of men* –   good-looking/handsome/striking/attractive   He's quite handsome.
He's a good-looking man.
– *of both* –   undistinguished/ordinary/unattractive/ugly

B8   Talking about someone's health

(*informal*)   Fine.   Fine, thanks.
She's as fit as a fiddle
She's in good shape.   Keeping well.
So so.   Middling.
A bit up and down.   Only fair.
Not too good.   Under the weather.
(*formal*)   Very/extremely well.
In good/excellent health.
Quite well.   In fair/average health.
Rather poorly.   Not very well at all.

B9   Expressing habitual actions

He smokes.   He smokes a lot.
He smokes all the time.
He smokes habitually/ceaselessly/incessantly/continually/continuously/night and day.   He's in the habit of smoking.
He never stops smoking.
He smokes and smokes and smokes.
He's a regular/perpetual smoker.
He's always smoking.
He's forever smoking.
He goes on/keeps on/carries on/continues smoking.

B10   Telling the time

It's one/two/three etc. o'clock.
It's midday (noon)/midnight.
quarter past two (two fifteen)

half past three (three thirty)
quarter to five (four forty-five)
five/ten/twenty/twenty-five past seven
five/ten/twenty/twenty-five to ten
but one minute/three minute/twelve minutes/twenty-four mintues past one
two five   two ten   two fifteen   two twenty
two twenty-five   two thirty   two thirty-five
two forty   two forty-five   two fifty
two fifty-five

C ATTITUDES

Feelings and emotions

C1 Saying what you like
I'm mad about wine.   I adore wine.
I really go for wine.
Wine is my big thing. (*informal*)
I love parties.   I enjoy parties.
I'm fond of chocolate.
I've got a weakness for chocolates.
I rather go for chocolates. (*informal*)
I quite like sport.
I don't mind classical music.
I can put up with classical music.

C2 Saying what you don't like
I'm not very keen on cheese.
I'm not a lover of cheese.
I'm not a cheese-lover.
Cheese is not my favourite food.
I don't like/I dislike heavy clothes.
Heavy clothes are unpleasant.
I hate work. Work is hateful.
I loathe the income-tax man.
I've got a loathing for income-tax men.
I detest the tax man.   He's detestable.
I can't stand politicians.
Politicians are intolerable.

C3 Expressing pleasure
I'm very glad/happy/pleased/thrilled to be here.
It gives me great pleasure/joy/happiness to be here.
I'm delighted/overjoyed.
It's very pleasing/pleasant/satisfying/ thrilling to be here.   I really like it here.
I want you to know how pleased etc. I am.
I'd like to express my great satisfaction/joy/ happiness/delight at being here. (*formal*)

C4 Sharing pleasure
Well done.   Congratulations.
I'm very happy etc. for you.
I share your pleasure/joy/happiness.
May I offer my congratulations.
I'd like to congratulate you.

C5 Showing displeasure
I'm (very) unhappy/displeased/annoyed/ dissatisfied/distressed/concerned/ disappointed/disturbed about it.
It causes me (great/considerable) unhappiness/displeasure/annoyance/ dissatisfaction/distress/concern/ disappointment/disturbance.
It is (very/most) displeasing/annoying/ distressing/disappointing/disturbing.
It displeases/annoys/distresses/concerns/ disturbs me.
I want you to know how unhappy I am about it.

C6 Expressing anger
I'm irritated/peeved/annoyed/cross/angry/ furious/incensed/vexed/nettled/displeased.
You've annoyed/angered/infuriated me.
He made me see red.   I flared up.
I lost my temper/cool.
He pushed me too far.
I was in a rage/temper/fury.
I was beside myself with rage.
I flew into a temper.
I'm mad.   I'm hopping mad.   I'm blazing.
I'm blazing mad.   I lost my cool. (*slang*)
I flew off the handle. (*slang*)

C7 Expressing sadness and grief
I'm upset/unhappy/sad/saddened/ sorrowful/miserable/wretched/dejected/ bitter about it.
It upsets/saddens/troubles/distresses/ grieves me.
It's upsetting/saddening/distressing.
I feel upset etc.
I'm gloomy/melancholy/mournful/downcast.
I'm cut up about it.   I'm low. (*informal*)
I'm in mourning for her.   I grieve for her.
I'm grief-stricken about her.
I'm sorrowful about it.
I've suffered a bereavement/loss.

C8 Breaking bad news
He's not very well/not too well/not on top/ rather under the weather/rather ill/going through a bad patch/having a rough time at the moment, I'm afraid.
I'm afraid I've got some rather serious news for you.
I'm afraid it doesn't look too good.
It's not very good news I've got for you.
I'm sorry/unhappy to say she's rather poorly.

Try to prepare yourself for a shock/some bad news/unwelcome news.
Now try to be brave because . . .
I'm going to have to ask you to be brave because . . .
I'd like to have/I wish I had better news for you, but . . .

C9 Expressing concern
I'm worried/concerned/bothered/dismayed/troubled about the news.
That's rather worrying.
I don't like to hear that.
I find that rather disturbing.

C10 Expressing regret
I'm sorry I did it.   I wish I hadn't done it.
I regret it.   I regret that I did it.
I regret doing it.   If only I hadn't done it.
Had I not done it, all would be well.
I feel regretful/remorseful that I did it/for doing it.   It's a matter of regret to me.
I'll always regret it.

C11 Expressing fear
I'm afraid/in fear/frightened/scared/terrified of being ill.
I'm nervous/anxious/alarmed about flying.
I've got a fear/terror of flying.
I'm in a panic/panic-stricken/frightened to death about my exam results.
I dread exams.
I'm in a state/dither/flap about being late. (*informal*)
I've got cold feet about the journey. (*informal*)
I've got the wind up about the journey. (*informal*)
Horror films make my blood run cold/make my flesh creep.   They scare/terrify/petrify me.

Allaying fear
Don't be afraid.   Don't worry.
There's no need to worry/to be concerned.
There's no cause for alarm/anxiety/concern.
I want to assure/reassure you.
You may rest assured.
Put your mind at rest.
Don't lose any sleep over it.
Try not to get into a state about it. (*informal*)

C12 Expressing guilt, confessing
I'm afraid/I have to admit/I must admit/I confess/I acknowledge/I must own up that I did it.
I've got something on my conscience I feel guilty about.

I need to talk about it/get if off my chest (*informal*)/relieve my conscience/come clean about it. (*informal*)
I'm sorry for/I regret/I'm ashamed of/I feel conscience-stricken about/feel guilty about doing it.

Modality

C13 Expressing possibility
Perhaps/Possibly/Probably/Maybe it's true.
It's possible that it's true.
There's a slight/good possibility that it's true.
It's probable that it's true.
There's a (strong) probability that it's true.
It's likely to be true/that it's true.
There's some likelihood that it's true.
It's not certain/There's no certainty that it's true.
It's uncertain/There's some uncertainty that it's true.
There's a small/good/strong chance that it's true.   The chances are good.
It's on the cards.   It's not to be ruled out.
It's not out of the question.
It may/might/could be true.
You can/are able to do it.
There's nothing to stop you doing it.
It can be done.

C14 Expressing impossibility
It's not possible.   It's impossible.
There's no possibility.   It's improbable.
It can't be true.   It's unlikely to be true.
There's no likelihood that it's true.
There's no way that it's true.
No way!   There's no chance.
It's out of the question.
It's not on. (*informal*)
You can't/aren't able to do it.
It can't be done.

C15 Expressing disbelief
That's impossible/incredible/unbelievable.
That's not true/possible/so/the case.
I question/doubt/challenge/refute/reject that idea.
You surely don't expect me to believe that.
I can't believe/accept/credit/take in the idea.
It's hard to believe/accept/credit/take in.
There must be a mistake/misunderstanding/something wrong.
Surely not.   It can't be, surely.
You're joking.   You're joking, of course.
You must be joking.
Surely that can't be right/true/so.

I wonder if that's right/true/so.
(*informal*)   Pull the other one.
Tell me another.   A likely story/tale.
That's a good one.
What a load of rubbish/old cobblers.
Nonsense.   Stuff and nonsense.   Rubbish.

C16 Expressing obligation/necessity
(*obligation*)   You must/ought to/should/have to/have got to go.
You'd better go.
You are obliged to go.
You have an obligation to go.
It is obligatory to go.
You are compelled to go.
It is compulsory to go.
(*necessity*)   You need to go.
You have a necessity to go.
It's necessary to go.
It's essential to go.
(*absence of obligation/necessity*)
You don't have to go.   You needn't go.
There's no need (for you) to go.
There's no necessity/It's not necessary to go.
You are not obliged/compelled to go.
There's no obligation/compulsion to go.
It's not obligatory/compulsory to go.
You are not forced/obliged to go.

C17 Expressing certainty and uncertainty
(*certainty*)   I'm certain/sure/positive/confident it is.   I've no doubt it is.
It's sure/certain/bound to be.
(There's) no doubt it is.
Without doubt/question it is.
Without a shadow of a doubt it is.
I bet it is.   You bet your life it is. (*informal*)
(*uncertainty*)   I don't know/can't think/can't imagine/can't decide what to do.
I'm trying to think/decide/make my mind up how to do it.   I'm uncertain/undecided/doubtful/hesitant about/not sure when to go.
I've no idea/I haven't a clue (*informal*)/I'm in a dither about (*informal*) where to go.
I've been racking my brains about/I'm wondering who to ask.

C18 Expressing determination
I will do it.   I'm determined/I resolve/I'm resolved/I intend/I've made up my mind to do it.   I'm firmly resolved to do it.
I've committed myself to do it.
My mind's made up. No-one can stop me.

C19 Expressing wishes
(*in the present*)   I wish he was sensible.
I wish I could swim.   If only he was sensible.
If only I could swim.
(*in the past*)   I wish he'd been sensible.
I wish I'd been able to swim.
If only he'd been sensible.
If only I'd been able to swim.
Had he been sensible, all would be well.
Had I been able to swim, all would be well.
(*in the future*)   I hope he's going to be sensible.   I'm dying to be able to go.
If only he'll be sensible.   If only I can go.

Personal relations

C20 Apologising
(*spoken*)   Sorry.   I'm sorry.
I'm very/so sorry.   I'm awfully sorry.
I'm terribly sorry.   It's all my fault.
I'm afraid I did it.   I'm sorry to say I did it.
I regret to say I did it.
I'm ashamed to say I did it.
My apologies.   My sincere apologies/regrets. (*formal*)
I do apologise.   Please accept my apologies.
Please excuse me.   Forgive me.
Please forgive me.
(*written*)   I must apologise for being late.
Please accept my apologies for being late.
I offer my apologies for being late.
It was my fault.
I was responsible for/I must accept responsibility for the accident.
The accident was my responsibility.
I beg your forgiveness/pardon for being rude.
I would like you to know how much I regret/deplore/feel ashamed about my actions.
I was filled with regret/overcome with remorse to hear how you felt.
I trust you will accept my most sincere apologies.
(*replying to apologies*)   That's all right.
It's nothing.   It doesn't matter.
Think no more about it.
Please don't apologise.
You needn't be sorry.

C21 Being confidential
Between ourselves ...
Between you and me ...
Between these four walls ...
Between friends ...
To tell you the truth ... To be truthful ...
To be honest ...   In all honesty ...
Quite honestly ...   In confidence ...
Confidentially ...
In the strictest confidence ...
To let you into a secret ...

To be completely open with you . . .
Frankly . . .   To be frank . . .

C22 Making promises
I promise/guarantee/swear/give an undertaking that I'll do it.
I agree/undertake to do it.
I assure you I will.
I can assure you that I will.
You may be assured that I will.
Please be assured that I will.
You have my assurance that I will.
I give you my word.   You can take my word.
Take my word.   Take it from me.
On my word of honour, I will.
There's no question that it's true.
There can be no question/doubt that it's true.
You can be certain that it's true.

C23 Seeking, giving and refusing permission
(*asking permission*)   May I go?
Please may I go?   Can I go?
Please can I go?   I'd like to go.
Do you mind if I go?
I hope you don't mind if I go.
If you don't mind, I'd like to go.
Have you any objections to me going?
Is there any reason why I can't/shouldn't go?
Will you allow/permit/authorise me to go?
Will you let me go?
Will you agree/consent to me going?
You won't refuse to let me go, will you?
You won't refuse to allow/permit/authorise me to go, will you?
You won't refuse to agree/consent to me going, will you?
Is it OK/all right to go?
Is it OK/all right by you if I go?
Is it acceptable to you if I go?
What would you say if I wanted to go?
Would you stop me going?
Would you refuse if I asked to go?
How about me going? (*informal*)
(*giving permission*)   Yes, you may/can go.
I don't mind if you go.
I don't mind you going.
I've no objection to you going.
I can't see any reason why you can't go.
Yes, I'll let you go.   I'm all in favour.
I'm all for it.   By all means.   Go ahead.
You have my permission/agreement/consent/authority/authorisation to go. (*formal*)
(*refusing permission*)   No, you can't/may not.
Certainly not.
Of course I mind/object/refuse.
I certainly will not agree/consent.
I certainly will not allow/permit/authorise it.
You don't go with my agreement/approval/permission/consent/blessing.
I'm sorry, but I can't agree/consent.
I'm sorry, but I can't allow/permit/authorise it.
Unfortunately, I have to say no.
Sorry, but no.
I'm really sorry but I'll have to say no.

C24 Expressing prohibition
No, you can't/may not/mustn't.
I won't let/allow you.
I forbid it.
I forbid you to do it.
It's not allowed/permitted.
It's forbidden/prohibited.
You mustn't do it.
You're not to do it.
You're not allowed to do it.
No smoking.   No smoking please.
Please do not smoke.
This is a no smoking area.
Don't walk on the grass.
Keep off the grass.
No dogs.   No dogs allowed.
(*weaker prohibition*)   You shouldn't/oughtn't/had better not do it.
I advise/warn you not to do it.
I wouldn't advise/encourage you to do it.
I wouldn't, if I were you.

C25 Making threats
If you don't stop, I'll go.   Unless you stop, I'll go.
Stop or I'll go.   Continue, and I'll go.
Don't you dare continue.
You'd better stop, or I'll go.

C26 Complaining
I've no wish to grumble/complain/be critical/find fault, but . . .
I've got a bone to pick with you. (*informal, half-friendly*)
I am (rather) disappointed/unhappy/displeased/annoyed about it.
I wish to record/express my disappointment/unhappiness/displeasure/annoyance about it. (*written formal*)
I want to complain/to make a complaint/to lodge a complaint about it.
I have a complaint to make about it.
I wish to protest/to make a protest about it.
I have a protest to make.
I really must protest.
I object to it.   I have several objections to it.

I have every objection to it.
I really must raise an objection.
I feel (very) strongly about it.   I must register the strength of my feeling about it.
(*answering a complaint*)   What's the matter/trouble/problem/difficulty?
What exactly is the matter etc.?
What seems to be the matter etc.?
How can I help you?

C27 Giving praise
Well done.   You've done (very) well.
That's very pleasing/good etc.
I want to compliment/commend/pay a tribute to you.
I said he'd done well.
I paid him a compliment.
I patted him on the back.
I gave him a pat on the back. (*informal*)
I applauded his work/efforts.
I spoke highly/well of him.
No praise is too high for him.
I can't speak too highly of him.

C28 Making suggestions
(*spoken or informal written*)   Let's do it.
Let's not do it.
I suggest/propose/vote we do it.
Why don't we do it?   We could do it.
How/What about doing it?   Shall we do it?
Don't you think we should do it?
What's wrong with doing it?
Doing it might be a good idea.
How do you feel about doing it?

(*written or formal spoken*)
I suggest/My suggestion is that we do it.
If you follow my suggestion, you will do it.
Let me put a suggestion to you.
Allow me to make a suggestion.
I'd like you to consider this.
You might think about this.
Have you thought about this?
I'd like to put it to you that you should go.
I'd like you to go.
I'd like to persuade you to go.

C29 Giving advice
My advice is to stop.
If you take my advice you will stop.
I advise you to stop.
My recommendation is to leave.
If you follow my recommendations, you will leave.   I recommend you to leave.
I must advise/warn you against staying.
I'd like to dissuade you from staying.
Can I advise/recommend/persuade you to apply.
In my opinion/It's my opinion that you should apply.
If I were you/If I were in your shoes I'd take it.
I think you should/ought to take it.

C30 Drinking someone's health
Cheers. (*v. common*)   Good health.
Happy days.   Good luck.
Here's to you/us etc.
Here's mud in your eye.
The skin off your nose. (*humorous*)
Bottoms up.

Lexicon

L1 PERSONAL ATTRIBUTES

L1.1 *Physical qualities*

L1.1.1 Physical strength
- N strength, power, stamina; toughness, sturdiness; resilience, staying power, endurance; health, vigour, agility
- A strong, powerful; tough, sturdy, robust; resilient, enduring; healthy, vigorous, agile
- V be strong etc.; strengthen, toughen, endure

L1.1.2 Physical energy
- N energy, life, force, vitality; might, potency, vigour, activity, dynamism; effort, violence
- A energetic, lively, forceful, vital; mighty, potent, vigorous, active, dynamic; violent
- V be energetic etc.; enliven, force, vitalise, invigorate, activate, make an effort

L1.1.3 Physical weakness
- N weakness, feebleness, helplessness, frailty, fragility, impotence; exhaustion, faintness, fatigue; lameness, sickliness, illness
- A weak, feeble, powerless, helpless; frail, fragile, impotent, delicate, puny; exhausted, faint, fatigued, crippled, lame; sick, sickly, ill, failing, unhealthy, in poor health
- V be weak etc., weaken, enfeeble, exhaust; faint; cripple, lame; sicken, fail

L1.1.4 Attractiveness
- N beauty, loveliness, prettiness, attraction, attractiveness, grace; smartness, elegance; fashion, grooming, neatness, tidiness
- A beautiful, gorgeous, lovely; good-looking, handsome; pretty, attractive, graceful; striking, shapely; smart, elegant, well-dressed, chic, fashionable, in fashion; well-groomed, neat, tidy, trim; spotless, immaculate

L1.1.5 Unattractiveness
- N ugliness, hideousness, ghastliness, unsightliness; homeliness, plainness; untidiness; dirt, stain
- A ugly, hideous, ghastly, unsightly; homely, plain; untidy, inelegant, badly-dressed, out of fashion, unfashionable, scruffy; dirty, stained

L1.2 *Qualities of character*

L1.2.1 Strength of character
- N integrity, virtue, morals, morality; honesty, frankness, openness; loyalty, reliability, diligence; bravery, courage; confidence, conviction, faith, fidelity, morale; positiveness, optimism; high-mindedness, strength of character
- A virtuous, moral; honest, frank, open; loyal, reliable, diligent; brave, courageous; confident, convincing, faithful, positive, optimistic; high-minded, incorruptible
- V be honest etc., moralise, strengthen, inspire, arouse, animate, enliven, quicken, vitalise, fortify, intensify, invigorate, stimulate, comfort

L1.2.2 Weakness of character
- N weakness, sin, immorality; dishonesty, cowardice, coward, furtiveness, disloyalty, unreliability, laziness, corruption, bribery; nervousness; faithlessness, infidelity, bad faith; pessimism; low-mindedness
- A weak, sinful, immoral; dishonest, cowardly, furtive, disloyal, unreliable, lazy, corrupt; nervous, faithless, unfaithful; pessimistic; low-minded
- V be weak etc., weaken, seduce, lead astray, corrupt, demoralise

L1.2.3 Positive personal qualities
- N spirit, enthusiasm, keenness, eagerness; activity, forcefulness, initiative; warmth, friendliness, sympathy, affection; commitment, cooperation; confidence, modesty
- A spirited, enthusiastic, keen, eager; active, forceful; warm, friendly, sympathetic, affectionate; committed, cooperative; confident, modest, unassuming
- V to be spirited etc., enthuse about, sympathise, cooperate

L1.2.4 Negative personal qualities
- N apathy, inaction, passivity, indifference;

coolness, detachment; over-confidence, immodesty, vanity, conceit
A apathetic, unenthusiastic, inactive, passive, indifferent; cool, unfriendly, detached, distant, aloof, uninvolved, uncommitted, laid back, uncooperative; over-confident, immodest, vain, conceited
V to be apathetic etc.

L1.2.5 Admirable qualities
N good, goodness, niceness, sweetness, gentleness, charm; excellence, greatness, grandeur; honour, virtue, nobility, worth, morality, ethics; selflessness, unselfishness; conscience, scruple
A good, nice, fair, pleasant, fine, suitable, agreeable, congenial, sweet, gentle, charming; excellent, splendid, superb; great, grand; super, smashing (*informal*); wonderful, marvellous, magnificent, terrific, glorious, splendid, sensational; honourable, virtuous, noble, worthy, moral, ethical, selfless, unselfish, conscientious, hard-working, scrupulous

L1.2.6 Undesirable qualities
N badness, nastiness, harm, selfishness, cruelty; offence, foulness, rottenness; evil, obscenity, wickedness, depravity, sin, naughtiness, mischief; wrong, immorality
A bad, nasty, harmful, selfish, cruel, offensive, foul, rotten, evil, obscene, wicked, depraved, sinful, sinister, naughty, mischievous; awful, horrible, terrible, shocking, ghastly, dreadful, frightful, appalling; wrong, immoral, un-scrupulous, unethical

L1.2.7 Truthfulness
N truth, truthfulness, honesty, frankness, sincerity, openness, candour, reliability, decency
A truthful, honest, frank, sincere, open, candid, straight, straightforward, reliable, decent
V to be truthful etc., rely (up)on

L1.2.8 Untruthfulness
N cunning, dishonesty, insincerity, stealth, craft, craftiness, trick, trickery, cheat, cheating, lie, lying, deceit, deceitfulness, treachery, pretence, betrayal
A cunning, dishonest, insincere, stealthy, crafty, tricky, cheating, lying, deceitful, treacherous
V to be cunning etc., trick, lie, cheat, deceive, betray

L1.2.9 Virtue
N virtue, morality, goodness, uprightness, honour, nobility; saint, saintliness, worthiness, conscience, conscientiousness, decency, modesty, politeness, courtesy, civility, generosity, kindness, honesty, truth, candour, sincerity, altruism, integrity; chastity; duty, obedience
A virtuous, moral, good, proper, upright, honourable, noble; saintly, angelic; worthy, conscientious, decent, modest, polite, courteous, civil, generous, kind; honest, truthful, candid, sincere, altruistic; chaste; dutiful, obedient; blameless, innocent, harmless
V to be virtuous etc.

L1.2.10 Vice
N vice, immorality, loose morals, wickedness, evil, sin, sinfulness, sinner; iniquity, wrong, guilt, badness, shamefulness, shamelessness; villainy, villain, misconduct, misbehaviour, delinquency, wrongdoing, wrongdoer, crime, criminal, transgression, misdeed; weakness, failing, fault, naughtiness
A vicious, immoral, loose, wicked, evil, sinful; wrong, guilty, bad, shameful; villainous, delinquent, criminal; weak, naughty
V to be vicious etc.

L1.2.11 Aggression
N aggression, offence, bullying, violent, wild, cruel, fierce, savagery; insult, abuse; rudeness, cheek, impudence, impertinence, insolence
A aggressive, offensive, bullying, violent, wild, cruel, fierce, savage; insulting, abusive; rude, cheeky, impudent, impertinent, insolent
V to be aggressive etc., assault, attack, bully; molest, offend, insult, abuse

L1.2.12 Crime and sins
N crime, criminal, sin, sinner, terrorism, terrorist; murder, murderer, killing, killer, destruction, destroyer, assassination, assassin, homicide; execution, executioner, massacre, suicide, bloodshed, extermination; butcher, cutthroat; theft, thief, stealing, robbery, robber, burglary, burglar, housebreaker; pickpocket, hold-up, smash and grab, pilfering, pilferer, poaching, poacher,

shop-lifting, shop-lifter, looting, looter; embezzlement, embezzler; fraud, swindle, swindler, confidence trickster; piracy, pirate, smuggling, smuggler; rape, rapist; arson, arsonist, fire-raising, fire-raiser; hijack, hijacker; blackmail, blackmailer; extortion; kidnapping, kidnapper; treachery, traitor; lie, lying, untruth, untruthfulness, white lie; cheating, cheat; adultery, adulterer; greed, avarice; bribery, corruption
A criminal, sinful, terrorist, murderous, destructive, homicidal, suicidal, thieving; fraudulent, piratical, extortionate; treacherous, traitorous; lying, untruthful, cheating; adulterous; greedy, avaricious; corrupt

L1.3 Emotions

L1.3.1 Strong feelings
N feeling, sentiment, emotion, passion; impulse, mood, sensation, thrill, exhilaration, enthusiasm, excitement, hysteria; favouritism, partiality, preference, bias, prejudice, aversion
A sentimental, emotional, passionate; impulsive, moody, sensational, thrilling, exhilarating, enthusiastic, exciting, excitable, excited, tense, on edge, worked-up, wound up, feverish, hysterical, over-wrought, highly strung, unstable; partial, biased, prejudiced
V to be sentimental etc.; feel, sense, thrill, enthuse, excite favour, prefer

L1.3.2 Absence of strong feeling
N disinterest, impartiality, neutrality, objectivity
A disinterested, impartial, neutral, objective, unbiased, unprejudiced; unmoved, uninfluenced, unflustered, unemotional, unenthusiastic, unhysterical, stable; laid back (*informal*), cool
V to be disinterested etc.

L1.3.3 Attraction
N attraction, appeal, fascination, enthralment, enchantment, charm, captivation, temptation, enticement, lure; concern
A attractive, appealing, fascinating, enthralling, enchanting, charming, captivating, tempting, enticing, alluring
V attract, appeal, fascinate, enthral, enchant, charm, captivate, tempt, entice, lure; concern

L1.3.4 Revulsion
N disgust, repulsion, revulsion, alienation, offence
A disgusting, repulsive, repellant, revolting, offensive; off-putting (*informal*)
V disgust, repulse, revolt, alienate, offend; put-off

L1.3.5 Emotional need
N want, desire, longing (for), craving (for). lust, yearning; hope, despair, desperation; greed, avarice; jealousy, envy, resentment
A lustful, yearnful; hopeful, despairing, desperate; greedy, avid, avaricious; jealous, envious, resentful
V want, desire, long (for), crave (for), covet, lust (after), yearn (for); hope, despair; envy, resent

L1.3.6 Liking
N admiration, respect; liking, fancy, care, fondness, keenness, attachment, attraction, love, adoration, ardour, doting, desire, lust
A admirable, respectable, respectful, respected, likeable, liked, fanciful, caring, fond, keen, attractive; lovable, adorable, desirable
V admire, respect, look up to, have a high opinion of, like, fancy, care for, be fond of/keen on/drawn to/attached to/attracted by, love, adore, dote upon, cherish, desire, lust after

L1.3.7 Disliking
N dislike; hatred, loathing, detestation, abhorrence, disregard, contempt
A disliked; hateful, loathsome, detestable, abhorrent, contemptible, contemptuous
V dislike; hate, loathe, detest, abhor; can't stand (*informal*), disregard, despise, look down on, have a low opinion of

L1.3.8 Friendly, supportive emotions
N compassion, pity, mercy, humanity, sympathy, tolerance, charity, leniency, generosity; condolence, consolation, solace, remorse; consideration, goodwill, kindness; friendship, favour, protection, patronage, benevolence
A compassionate, pitiful, merciful, humane, sympathetic; tolerant, charitable, lenient, generous; remorseful; considerate, consolatory; friendly, favourable, protective, benevolent
V pity, sympathise, tolerate; condole,

console, solace; befriend, favour, protect, patronise

L1.3.9 Unfriendly, unsupportive emotions
N   unkindness, intolerance; hostility, antagonsim, antipathy, animosity, malevolence
A   unkind, intolerant, merciless, pitiless, ruthless, remorseless, heartless, unsympathetic, resentful; inimical, hostile antagonistic, malevolent
V   be intolerant etc.

L1.3.10 Happiness
N   happiness, gladness, pleasure, cheerfulness, enjoyment, joy, elation, delight, euphoria; merriment, gaiety, jollity; satisfaction, contentment, wellbeing; gratitude, thankfulness
A   happy, glad, pleased, cheerful, enjoyable, joyful, elated, delighted, euphoric; merry, gay, jolly, overjoyed; satisfied, content, contented; grateful, thankful
V   be happy etc., enjoy, rejoice, delight, take pleasure, please, satisfy, content

L1.3.11 Sadness
N   sadness, sorrow, care, unhappiness, concern, boredom; misery, wretchedness, woe, mournfulness, grief, distress; pathos, depression, remorse, regret, disappointment; embarrassment, humiliation, shame, disgrace, guilt
A   sad, sorry, sorrowful, care-worn, unhappy, concerned, bored; joyless, miserable, wretched, woeful, mournful, grief-stricken, heart-broken, harrowing, distressed, distressing; pathetic, depressed, fed up, remorseful, regretful, disappointed, disappointing; embarrassed, embarrassing, humiliated, humiliating, ashamed, shameful, disgraced, disgraceful, guilty
V   be unhappy etc., sadden, sorrow, bore, mourn, grieve, regret, disappoint, embarrass, humiliate, shame, disgrace

L1.3.12 Anger
N   irritation, displeasure, annoyance, resentment, anger, wrath, fury, rage, temper
A   nettled, irritated, displeased, annoyed, resentful, peevish, fretful, cross, angry, wrathful, furious, enraged, mad, maddened, irritable, irate
V   nettle, irritate, displease, annoy, resent, peeve, fret, infuriate, enrage, madden, to be nettled etc.

L1.3.13 Excitement
N   interest, excitement, thrill, stimulus, stimulation, enthusiasm
A   interesting, interested, excited, excitable, thrilled, thrilling, stimulated, keen, fascinated, enthusiastic, breath-taking

L1.3.14 Tension
N   excitement, tension, stress, suspense, hysteria, hysterics; astonishment, amazement
A   excited, excitable, tense, stressful, hysterical; astonished, astonishing, startled, startling, astounded, astounding, amazed, amazing, appalled, appalling
V   excite, tense, surprise, astonish, startle, astound, amaze, take aback, appall

L1.3.15 Absence of tension
N   quiet, quietness, calm, calmness, patience, peace, peacefulness, tranquillity, serenity, relaxation, comfort, ease
A   quiet, calm, patient, peaceful, tranquil, serene, relaxed, comfortable, snug
V   quieten, calm, tranquilise, relax, comfort, calm down, cool down, ease, comfort

L1.3.16 Fear
N   timidity, nervousness, anxiety, alarm; fear, fright, terror, horror, coward, cowardice
A   timid, nervous, anxious, alarmed; fearful, frightened, terrified, terrifying, terrible, horrifed, horrifying, horrible, horrendous, scared; cowardly

L1.3.17 Bravery
N   bravery, courage, boldness, spirit, heroism, daring, valour, gallantry; audacity, nerve, cheek; recklessness, rashness
A   brave, courageous, bold, spirited, heroic, daring, valorous, gallant; audacious, cheeky; reckless, rash
V   to be brave etc.

L1.3.18 Emotional communication
N   pride, conceit, vanity, arrogance, snobbery; boast, boasting, bragging, braggart, showing off, swank, swanking, crowing; insistence, demand, argument; pleading, appeal; complaint, protest, objection, grumble, grouse, moan; accusation, blame, condemnation; admission, confession, concession, acknowledgement; warning, threat,

blackmail; scorn, scoffing, mockery, sneer, jeer, ridicule; insult, affront, humiliation, derision; denunciation, curse, damnation
A proud, conceited, vain, arrogant, snobbish; boastful, bragging, swanking, crowing; insistent, demanding, argumentative; beseeching, entreating, imploring, pleading, appealing; complaining, protesting, objecting, objectionable, grumbling, grousing, moaning; accusing, blaming, blameful, condemning, condemned; admitted, admissible, confessed, conceded, acknowledged; warning, threatening, blackmailing; scornful, scoffing, mocking sneering, jeering, ridiculous; insulting, humiliating; cursed, damned
V boast, brag, show off, swank, crow; insist, demand, argue; beseech, entreat, implore, plead, appeal to; complain, protest, object, grumble, grouse, moan; accuse, blame, condemn; admit, confess, concede, acknowledge, warn, threaten, blackmail; scorn, scoff, mock, sneer, jeer, ridicule; insult, affront, humiliate, deride; denounce, curse, damn

L1.4 *Thinking and knowing*

L1.4.1 Intellect
N brain, mind, thought, intelligence; reason, mentality, wisdom; logic, reasoning, idea, concept, brainwave, imagination, dream, fancy; guess, notion, impression, opinion; theory, hypothesis, deduction, conclusion
A brainy, mindful, thoughtful, intelligent, reasoned; mental, wise; logical, conceptual, imagined, imaginative, dreamy, fanciful; notional, impressionable; theoretical, hypothetical, deductive, conclusive
V think, reason, conceive; theorise, hypothesise, deduce, conclude; imagine, dream, fancy

L1.4.2 Understanding
N knowledge, awareness, consciousness; recognition, comprehension, realisation; understanding, certainty, appreciation, grasp, identification, identity; training, education, teaching, instruction, coaching, tuition; information, warning, suggestion, familiarity, acquaintance
A known, knowledgeable, aware, sensitive, recognisable, comprehensible; appreciative, identifiable; trained, educated, educational, teaching, instructive, instructional, coaching; informative, well-informed, familiar, conversant with, acquainted with
V know, sense, recognise, comprehend, realise, understand, be certain, appreciate, grasp, identify; train, educate, teach, instruct, coach; inform, warn, suggest, familiarise, acquaint

L1.4.3 Judgement
N judgement, assessment, analysis; reckoning, calculation, estimate, estimation; criticism, interpretation; belief, acceptance, impression; accusation, blame, criticism, inquiry
A analytical, critical; believable, acceptable, credible, impressed, impressive; accused, blamed, critical
V judge, assess, analyse; reckon, calculate, estimate, determine; criticise, weigh up, interpret; believe, accept, credit, impress; accuse, blame, criticise, inquire

L1.4.4 Misjudgement
N misjudgement, miscalculation, misunderstanding, misinterpretation; prejudice, predisposition, bias; under/over-estimation
A misjudged, miscalculated, misunderstood, misinterpreted; prejudged, prejudiced, predisposed, biased; under/over-estimation
V misjudge, miscalculate, misunderstand, misinterpret; prejudge, predispose, take sides, be biased; under/over-estimate

L1.4.5 Positive intellectual qualities
N intelligence, cleverness, brains, brilliance, brightness; shrewdness, smartness; wit, wisdom, caution; ingenuity; genius, sense, ability, capability, skill, talent, gift, proficiency, aptitude, flair
A intelligent, clever, brainy, brilliant, bright; shrewd, smart; wise, witty, cautious; ingenious, sensible, able, capable, skilful, talented, gifted, proficient, apt
V be intelligent etc.

L1.4.6 Negative intellectual qualities
N slowness, dullness, stupidity, backwardness; idiot, fool, folly, clown; ignorance; madness, madman, lunacy, lunatic, insanity, imbecile, imbecility
A slow, dull, stupid, backward, retarded, thick (*informal*); idiotic, silly, foolish, daft

(*informal*), barmy (*informal*), batty (*informal*), brainless, mindless; ignorant; mad, crazy, lunatic, insane, imbecile, unbalanced, nuts (*informal*), off one's head/rocker (*informal*), out of one's mind
V to be slow etc., to have bats in the belfry (*informal*)

L1.4.7 Knowledge
N Knowledge, experience; awareness, consciousnes, familiarity; information, acquaintance
A known, experienced; aware of, conscious of, conversant with, familiar with; informed, acquainted with
V know, experience; make aware of/conscious of/conversant with, familiarise; inform, acquaint with

L1.4.8 Lack of knowledge
N ignorance, inexperience; unawareness, unconsciousness, unfamiliarity; innocence, simplicity; uncertainty, doubt
A ignorant, inexperienced; unaware, unconscious of, unfamiliar with; innocent, simple; uncertain, doubtful, unknown; uneducated, untrained, untaught, uninformed
V to not know, be in the dark, be innocent of; forget, ignore, desregard; misunderstand; doubt

L1.4.9 Seeking knowledge
N discovery, discoverer, notice, detection, investigation, investigator; study, student; question, wonder, doubt, suspect, suspicion, pondering; reflection, meditation, contemplation
A discovered, spotted, detected; investigative, studious; questioned, questionable, doubted, doubtful, suspicious; reflected, contemplated, contemplative
V find out, discover, notice, spot, detect; investigate, study, question, wonder, doubt, suspect; ponder, reflect, mediate, contemplate

L1.4.10 Reasoning
N reason, argument, debate, discussion, conclusion, inference, deduction, assumption, presumption, proof; supposition, reckoning, calculation; guess, theory, consideration; agreement, admission, concession, grant; decision, choice, option, selection
A reasonable, argumentative, conclusive, deductive, proven; supposed, reckoned, calculated, guessed, theoretical, considered; agreed, admitted, conceded, granted; decided, chosen, opted, selected
V reason, argue, debate, discuss, conclude, infer, deduce, gather, assume, presume, prove; suppose, reckon, calculate, guess, theorise, consider; agree, admit, concede, grant; decide, choose, opt for, select

L1.4.11 Belief
N Belief, believer, faith, credence, creed, conviction, certainty, acceptance; agreement, assumption, supposition; conviction, assurance, reassurance, confidence; impression
A believing, believable, faithful, convinced, certain; acceptable, agreeable; confident
V believe, credit, accept; admit, agree; assume, suppose, acknowledge; convince, assure, reassure; confide in, impress

L1.4.12 Lack of belief
N disbelief, doubt, uncertainty; disagreement; criticism
A unbelieving, unbelievable, doubting, doubtful, incredible, uncertain; unacceptable, unconvinced, incredulous; critical
V disbelieve, doubt, question, deny; lack confidence/conviction; criticise

L1.4.13 Thinking ahead
N anticipation, forethought, premeditation; intention, preparation; expectation, expectancy; foresight, vision, visionary, foretelling, fortune, fortune-teller, astrology, astrologer, prediction, forecast, forecaster; prophet, prophecy, horoscope, foreboding, omen; planning, hope, concept, projection; ambition, aspiration; reservation, booking, arrangement, registration; fate, destiny, doom, condemnation; warning sign, omen; indication, promise, pledge, guarantee, undertaking, notice, notification, advertisement; aim, goal, target, object, end, quarry, winning post, intent, intention; purpose, resolve, resolution, design, desire, proposal, deferment, postponement; want, desire, longing; plot, scheme, design, plan, planner, draft, rehearsal, readiness; savings, hoard, nest-egg, store, storage, reserves, stock, collection
A anticipated, anticipatory, expected,

foreseen, foretold, predicted, ominous; planned, conceptual, ambitious, reserved, booked, arranged, registered; fated, destined, doomed, condemned, ordained; potential, imminent, forthcoming, impending, indicated, promised, pledged, guaranteed, notified, advertised; intended, intentional, purposed, designed, desired, proposed, deferred, postponed; plotted, schemed, planned, drafted, rehearsed, ready; saved, hoarded, stored, reserved, stocked, collected

V anticipate, look forward, look ahead, expect, foresee, foretell, predict, forecast, prophesy, forebode, look forward to, plan, hope, envisage, conceive, project, aspire; reserve, book, arrange, earmark, register; doom, condemn, ordain; warn, signify, indicate; promise, pledge, guarantee, undertake, give notice, notify, advertise; intend, purpose, aim at, resolve, propose, defer, put off, postpone; pursue, have designs on; plot, scheme, design, plan, draft, rehearse, make ready, get ready; save, hoard, put by, store, reserve, stock, collect

L1.4.14 Thinking back
N retrospect, retrospection, reflection, recall, recollection, remembrance, memory, reminiscence; dream dreaming, reverie; regret
A retrospective, reflective, recalled, recollected, remembered, reminiscent; dreamy; regretful
V look back, reflect, recall, recollect, remember, bring to mind, reminisce; dream; regret

L1.5 *Opinion*
L1.5.1 Idea
N idea, concept, conception, belief, attitude, view, viewpoint, perception, comprehension, grasp, theory, hypothesis; regard, consideration, opinion, judge, judgement, verdict, decision, advice; appraisal, evaluation, assessment, assessor; interpretation, appreciation, analysis, arbitration, diagnosis, conclusion, consensus; sentiment; bigotry, bigot
A conceptual, perceptive, comprehensible; theoretical, hypothetical; considered, opinionated, judicial, decisive, advisory; interpretative, appreciative; analytical, arbitrary; diagnostic, conclusive; sentimental; bigoted
V conceptualise, believe; view, perceive, comprehend, grasp; theorise, hypothesise; regard, consider; judge, decide, advise; appraise, evaluate, assess; interpret, appreciate; analyse, arbitrate, diagnose, conclude

L1.5.2 Forming opinions
N assumption, supposition, imagination; deduction, conclusion, inference interpretation, reason; debate, discussion, argument; influence, moulding, impression, guidance, manipulative, brain-washing, indoctrination; conviction, persuasion, dissuasion, (re)assurance; coaxing, flattery; suggestion, hint, proposal
A assumed, supposed, imagined, imaginary; deductive, conclusive, inferential. interpretative, reasoned; debated, argumentative; influential, impressive, guided, manipulative, convincing, persuasive, dissuasive, (re)assuring, coaxing, flattering; suggestive, suggestible, hinted, proposed
V assume, suppose, imagine; deduce, conclude, infer, interpret, reason; debate, discuss, argue; influence, mould, impress; guide, manipulate, brain-wash, indoctrinate; convince, persuade, dissuade, (re)assure; coax, flatter; suggest, hint, propose

L1.5.3 Sharing an opinion
N agreement, harmony, concord; consent, unanimity; support, supporter, second, seconder, assent, assentor, follower; abettor, subscriber, acceptance, faith, credulity
A agreed, harmonious; unanimous; supporting, supportive; accepted
V agree, harmonise; consent, support, second, assent, follow; abet; subscribe, accept, believe

L1.5.4 Not sharing an opinion
N disagreement, difference of opinion, rejection, disapproval; protest, dissent, discord, hostility; misgiving, mistrust, doubt, doubter, scepticism, sceptic, agnosticism, agnostic, disbelief, disbeliever, unbeliever
A disregard, rejected, disapproved; discordant, hostile; mistrusted, doubted,

doubtful, sceptical, agnostic, disbelieving
V   disagree, differ, reject, disapprove; protest, dissent; misgive, mistrust, doubt, disbelieve

L1.5.5 Positive opinion
N   approval, appreciation, recognition, admiration, esteem, respect; praise, compliment, applause, acclaim, support
A   approving, appreciative, recognised, admired, esteemed, respected, respectful; praised, complimented, complimentary, applauded, acclaimed, supported, supportive
V   approve, appreciate, recognise, admire, esteem, respect; praise, compliment, applaud, acclaim, support

L1.5.6 Negative opinion
N   disapproval, rejection, disfavour, poor/low opinion, hostility, enmity, censure, blame, accusation, fault-finding, criticism, reproach, sneer, reprimand, rebuke
A   disapproving, rejected, unfavourable; hostile; censorious, censured, blamed, accused; critical, reproachful, sneering, reprimanded, rebuked
V   disapprove, reject, disfavour, have a poor/low opinion; censure, blame, accuse, find fault, criticise, reproach, sneer at, reprimand, rebuke, be hostile etc.

L1.6 Attitudes

L1.6.1 Positive attitudes to people
N   friend, friendship, ally, allegiance, pal, comrade, comradeship, colleague, mate, partner, supporter, support; kindness, goodness, goodwill, humanity, consideration, generosity, understanding, support, loyalty, fidelity, trust, uprightness, constancy, politeness
A   friendly, sociable, amiable, amicable, close, warm, cordial, easy, agreeable, kind, kindly, considerate, generous, understanding, supportive, loyal, trusting, constant
V   befriend, make friends (with), pal up with, support, agree, consider, understand, trust

L1.6.2 Negative attitudes to people
N   enemy, foe, opponent, hostility, antagonist, antagonism, disagreement, rudeness; unkindness, illwill, inhumanity, dishonesty, deceit, disloyalty, treachery, betrayal, infidelity, inconstancy, mistrust, impoliteness
A   unfriendly, unsociable, hostile, antagonistic, disagreeable, impolite, rude; unkind, inhuman, dishonest, deceitful, disloyal, treacherous, faithless, unfaithful, inconstant, mistrusting
V   disagree, oppose, be unfriendly etc.

L1.7 Communication

L1.7.1 General
N   language, meaning, significance; message, information; contact, transmission, data, news, bulletin; messenger, courier, runner, signaller, informant, speaker, spokesman, announcer; witness, spy; question, answer
A   linguistic, meaningful, significant, informative; transmitted
V   communicate, mean, signify, inform, tell, contact, transmit, signal; address, speak, announce, say; witness, spy; question, answer

L1.7.2 Spoken communication
N   word, message, messenger, speech, speaker, chat, chatterer, gossip, rumour, declaration, talk, talker; lecture, lecturer, discussion, debate, debater; narration, narrator, statement, announcement, announcer; oath; warning, advice, adviser, notice, mention, hint, confidence, confidante, indiscretion, whisper, suggestion, clue; call, caller, phone call, ring, dial
A   wordy, spoken, narrative, stated, announced; advised, noticed, notified, mentioned, hinted, confidential, indiscreet, whispered, suggested, suggestive
V   say, speak, chat, gossip, declare, narrate, state, announce; lecture, discuss, debate; tell, talk, repeat, disclose, inform, warn, advise, mention, hint, confide, whisper, suggest, proclaim, express, remark, comment, observe, protest, maintain, allege, swear, promise, offer, challenge, deny, refuse; agree; stress; confess, admit; ask, question, seek; call, phone, ring, dial

L1.7.3 Non-spoken communication
N   letter, card, mail, post, correspondence; post office, letter box, post box, pillar box, postman; writer, author, composer; document, note, file, record, report, paper, account, hand-out; advertisement,

publication, notification, headline, bill-board, hoarding, placard; broadcast, transmission, programme, radio, television, telephone, telegram, teleprinter, telex, record, recording
A written, posted, postal, composed, documentary, recorded, reported; advertised, published, notified; broadcast, transmitted, televised, telephonic, recorded; signalled, gestured
V write, send a letter, get in touch, drop a line, jot down, note down; post, deliver, despatch, remit; publish, print; signal, sign, gesture, gesticulate, wave, transmit, broadcast, televise, relay, record, tape; nod, wink, nudge, kick

L1.8.1 Family relationships
N relationship, kinship, parentage, descent, kinsman, relation, relative, next of kin; twin, brother, sister, cousin, uncle, aunt, nephew, niece, father, mother, parent, child; family, motherhood, fatherhood, brotherhood, sisterhood, foster-son, stepson, god-parent, in-laws; race, line, tribe, nation
A maternal, paternal, fraternal, brotherly, sisterly, related, next of kin
V father, mother, adopt

L2 NON-PERSONAL ATTRIBUTES

L2.1 *Relationships*

L2.1.1 Relationship
N relation, respect, involvement, relationship, association, intimacy, connection; link, bond, correlation, correspondence; equality, similarity, comparison; nearness, proportion, ratio, scale, cause; sequence, agreement, reference
A relative, respective, related, connected; concerning, belonging, mutual, reciprocal; like, similar, comparative, near, parallel, proportional, relevant, appropriate
V be related, have a relation, have reference, refer to, influence, touch, concern, deal with, affect; belong, correspond, reciprocate, correlate, be relevant, come to the point; relate, connect, apply, link, tie, compare, liken, parallel, equalise, refer to

L2.1.2 Non-relationship
N independence, freedom, isolation, separation; speciality, inequality, diversity, of no concern, no business; misfit, irrelevance, pointlessness, inconsequence; contrast
A unrelated, absolute, independent, free, isolated, alone, uninvolved, unconnected; individual, private, inappropriate, unequal, distorted, irrelevant, pointless; misplaced, misdirected, contrasting
V be unrelated etc., have no concern with, be off the point, contrast

L2.1.3 Correlation
N correlation, relation, proportion, correspondence, interrelation, interplay, reciprocity, reciprocation, interchange
A relative, reciprocal, corresponding, proportional, proportionate; mutual, alternating, alternate, interlocking, interacting, interchangeable, exchangeable
V correlate, interrelate, interconnect, interlock, interact, reciprocate, correspond, react; exchange, swop, barter, trade, balance, equalise, compensate

L2.1.4 Sameness
N identity, unity, similarity, identification, equality, uniformity, constancy; stability, regularity, unison, agreement, sameness; resemblance, likeness, analogy, equality, symmetry, comparison, imitation, parallel, equivalent, image; tolerance
A identical, same, similar, invariable, constant, unchangeable, uniform; consistent, fixed, unchanging, unbroken, monotonous; standard, normal, regular, straight; resembling, matching, equal, imitative, tolerant
V be identical, be the same; repeat, coincide, identify; equalise, equate, match, pair, liken; be uniform, resemble, reflect, imitate, look alike, take after, correspond to; tolerate

L2.1.5 Difference
N difference, opposition, disagreement, contest, combat, discord; contrast, variation, contradiction, distinction; opposite, extreme, reverse, converse; inconstancy, inconsistency, diversity, variety, mixture, unlikeness, inequality, variation; foreigner, alien, stranger; rival, competitor, antagonist, antagonism, hostility, belligerence

A contrary, different, contrasting, negative, discordant, opposite, reverse, converse, opposing; variable, inconsistent, irregular, uneven, dissimilar, divergent, unlike, unequal; foreign, alien, strange; competitive, rival, antagonistic, hostile, belligerent

V be different, be contrary, differ, contrast; disagree, clash, run counter; argue, oppose, combat, contest, contradict; distinguish; negate, reverse; be unlike, have nothing in common, differentiate; distort, alienate, estrange; compete, rival, antagonise

L2.1.6 Copy
N imitation, copy; rivalry, competition; reflection, mirror, echo, shadow; forgery, fake, falsehood; duplication, reproduction; mimicry, satire, mockery, imitation, imitator, ape, sheep, flatterer, yes-man; replica, likeness, similarity, image, duplicate, photography, photocopy, model

A imitative, apish, counterfeit, duplicate

V imitate, ape, copy, echo, mirror, reflect, resemble; parody, simulate, draw, trace, repeat, reproduce; transcribe, do likewise, follow suit, understudy

L2.1.7 Equality
N equality, sameness, balance, evenness, uniformity, identity, equivalence, six of one and half a dozen of the other; steadiness, equation; draw, tie, dead heat, equal match

A equal, same, identical, like, similar, agreeing, even, level, uniform; matched, parallel, on a par, comparable

V be equal, equal, coincide, accord, keep up with, tie, draw, break even; equalise, balance; mirror, reflect, resemble

L2.2   Control

L2.2.1   General control
N control, controller, influence, hold, management, manager, government, governor, discipline, rule, ruler, regulation, law, command, commander, commandment, dominion, domination, dominance, assertion, pressure, oppression, oppressor; persuasion, force, compulsion, prejudice, bias, brain-washing

A controlled, influential, managed, managerial, governmental, disciplinary, regulatory, legal; dominant, assertive, oppressive, persuasive, forceful, compelling, compulsive, prejudical

V control, influence, have a hold on, be listened to, manage, govern, discipline, rule, regulate; command, dominate, assert oneself, put pressure on, pull strings; persuade, prevail upon, convince, force, compel, prejudice, bias, brainwash

L2.2.2   Restraint
N restraint, self-restraint, holding back, hindrance, self control, check, rein, brake, halt; veto, ban, bar, prohibition, restriction; limitation, limit, moderation; repression, suppression; silence, gag; patrol, blockade; discipline, compulsion, police; arrest, capture, prison, prisoner, imprisonment, detention, custody, internment; bondage, bind, chain, cage, kennel, pen, lock-up, confinement; punishment, whipping, corrective, correction

A restrained, hindered, controlled, checked, reined in, braked, halted; vetoed, banned, barred, prohibited, prohibitive, restricted, restrictive; limited, repressed, suppressed; silenced, gagged; blockaded, disciplined, disciplinary; arrested, captured, captive, imprisoned, detained, bound, chained, caged, penned, locked-up, confined; punished, punitive, whipped, corrected, corrective

V restrain, hold back, retard, hinder, check, brake, rein in, halt; veto, ban, bar, prohibit; hold in, restrict, limit, moderate; repress, suppress; silence, gag; keep in; patrol, blockade; keep order, discipline, drill, compel, police; arrest, catch, capture, take prisoner, take into custody, intern; bind, chain, tie up; imprison, detain, enclose, cage, kennel, pen, shut in, shut up, lock up, confine; punish, whip, correct, subdue

L2.2.3   Management
N management, manager, manipulation, string pulling, handling, handler; conduct, running, administration, administrator; dealer, supervision, supervisor, oversee, oversight; order, regulation, authority, government, power, rule, ruler, reign; organiser, arranger; direction, director, lead, leader, leadership, command, commander, master, mastery, head, steering, navigation, navigator, conduct,

conductor, indication, indicator, guide, guidance, training, monitor; dictator, dictatorship
A managed, manipulated, manipulative, handled, conducted, administered, administrative, supervised, supervisory; ordered, regulated, regulatory, authoritarian, governing, reigning; organised, organisational, arranged; directional, navigational, indicatory, dictatorial
V manage, manipulate, pull strings, handle, conduct, run, carry on, administrator, deal with, cope with, see to, supervise, superintend, oversee; keep order, regulate, authorise, govern, rule, reign; organise, arrange, direct, lead, head, command, master, steer, navigate, conduct; indicate, guide, train, monitor; dictate

L2.2.4 Influence
N influence, command, domination, dominance, assertion, pressure; motivation, effect, impression, inspiration, persuasion; conviction, compulsion, force
A influential, commanding, dominating, assertive, pressed; motivating, effective, impressive, inspiring, inspired, persuasive; prevalent; convincing, convinced, compelling, forced, forceful
V influence, command, dominate, assert oneself, put pressure on, pressurise, pull strings; motivate, affect, impress, inspire, persuade; prevail upon, convince, compel, force

L2.2.5 Development
N development, improvement, enhancement, betterment, progress, expansion, rally, restoration, ascent, increase, revival, refreshment, stability, stabiliser
A developed, improved, enhanced, bettered, progressive, expanded, expansive, rallying, restored, increased, revived, refreshed, stable
V develop, improve, enhance, advance, better, progress, expand, rally, restore, ascend, increase, revive, refresh, stabilise

L2.3 *Movement*

L2.3.1 Motion
N move, movement, motion, stir, travel, conveyance; entry, entrance, crossing, emergence, dismissal; passage, fall, rise, jump, spin, shake, slide; shift, variation
A moving, travelling, travel, entering, crossing, settling, emerging, emergent, dismissed; passing, falling, rising, jumping, spinning, shaking, sliding; shifting, varying
V move, stir, travel, convey, enter, cross, settle, emerge, dismiss; pass, fall, rise, jump, spin, shake, slide; shift, vary

L2.3.2 Travel
N travel, traveller, journey, tour, tourist, tourism, visit, visitor, exploration, explorer, sightseeing, sightseer; passage, passenger, migration, migrant, emigration, emigrant, immigration, immigrant; cruise, cruiser, voyage, progression; ride, rider, drive, driver, sail, sailor, float, drifter; flying, flyer, soaring, touch-down; arrival, departure, meeting
A travelling, journeying, touring, visiting, on the road, sightseeing; passing, migrating, migratory, peripatetic; riding, driving, sailing, floating, drifting, landing; flying, soaring; arriving, departing, departure, meeting
V travel, journey, tour, see the world, visit, explore, sightsee; pass, migrate, emigrate, immigrate, cruise, voyage, progress; ride, drive, sail, put to sea, set sail, float, drift, land; fly, soar, take off, land, touch down; arrive, depart, meet

L2.3.3 Movement on foot
N walk, stroll, ramble, hike, march; pace, step, stride; run, jog, trot, canter, gallop, sprint; paddle, wade; limp, hobble, waddle; climb, scramble; dance, hop, glide; hurry, scurry, hasten, rush, dash, charge, race; strut, swagger
A walking, wandering, strolling, stepping, hiking, marching; pedestrian; running, jogging, skipping, trotting, cantering, galloping, striding; paddling, wading; climbing, dancing, creeping, rushing, dashing, racing; strutting, swaggering, mincing
V walk, amble, wander, saunter, stroll, ramble, hike, tramp, march; pace, step, stride; run, jog, skip, trot, canter, gallop, sprint; paddle, wade; limp, stagger, hobble, totter, waddle, stumble; climb, scramble, mount; dance, hop, glide, tiptoe, creep, sidle; hurry, scurry, hasten, rush, dash, charge, race, strut, swagger, mince

L2.3.4 Transference
- **N** transfer, delivery, conveyance, carriage; transmission; export, import; transport, transportation; move, movement, shifting, shift; ferry, ship, shipping, plane, car, lorry, truck, train; cargo, freight, passenger; post, mail, remittance; despatch
- **A** transferable, transferred, delivered, conveyed, carried; transmitted; exported, imported; transported, portable; moved, moveable, shifted; postage, posted, mailed, remitted; despatched
- **V** transfer, deliver, convey, carry; transmit, pass on; export, import, transport, move, shift; ferry, ship; post, remit; send, despatch, direct, post, forward

L2.3.5 Movement forwards and backwards
- **N** advance, advancement, procession, procedure, progress, progression, approach; retreat, retirement, relapse, reverse, reversal, backing, withdrawal; removal; shuttle
- **A** advancing, advanced, proceeding, progressing, progressive, approaching; retreating, retreated, retiring, retired, relapsing, relapsed, reversing, reversed, backing, withdrawing, withdrawn; removing, removed
- **V** advance, go on, move forward, proceed, progress, go ahead, approach; retreat, retire, go back, move back, recede, relapse, reverse, back, withdraw, give way, remove; shuttle

L2.3.6 Push and pull movement
- **N** push, launch, projection, throw, heave, toss, drive, kick, roll; repulsion, dispersal, rejection; pull, drag, draw, tug, tow, haul, haulage, lift, extraction; attraction, magnet, magnetism, appeal, temptation
- **A** pushing, pushed, launching, launched, projecting, projected, throwing, thrown, heaving, tossing, tossed, driving, driven, kicking, kicked, rolling, rolled; repelling, repelled, dispersing, dispersed, rejected; pulling, pulled, dragging, dragged, drawing, towing, towed, hauled, lifting, lifted, extracted; attracting, attractive, magnetic, appealing, tempting
- **V** push, launch, project, throw, heave, toss, fling, drive, kick, roll; turn away, send off, repel, disperse, snub, reject; pull, drag, draw, tug, tow, haul, trail, wind in, wind up, lift, extract; attract, magnetise, appeal, tempt

L2.3.7 Shaking movement
- **N** shake, vibration, sway, nod, swing, stagger, rock, wobble, wag, wave, flutter, tremble, shiver, wriggle, flap, twitch, blink
- **A** shaking, shaken, vibrating, vibrated, swaying, swayed, nodding, nodded, swinging, swung, staggering, staggered, rocking, rocked, wobbling, wobbled, wagging, wagged, waving, waved, fluttering, fluttered, trembling, trembled, shivering, shivered, wriggling, wriggled, flapping, flapped, twitching, twitched, blinking, blinked
- **V** shake, vibrate, sway, nod, swing, stagger, rock, wobble, wag, wave, flutter, tremble, shiver, wriggle; flap, twitch, blink

L2.4 Up and down

L2.4.1 Ascent
- **N** ascent, rise, climb, climbing, clambering, uprising, upsurge, take-off, flying, mounting, soaring, surfacing, rocketing
- **A** ascending, ascendant, rising, climbing, flying, mounting, soaring, surfacing, rocketing
- **V** ascend, rise, climb, clamber, scale, take off, fly, mount, soar, surface, rocket

L2.4.2 Descent
- **N** descent, fall, drop, tumble, sinking, slump, settling, gravitation, submergence, dive, plunge, dip, recession; burrowing, tunnelling, undermining; alighting, dismounting, disembarking, perching, landing, settling, touching down, swooping
- **A** descending, falling, fallen, dropping, tumbling, sinking, settling, submerging, diving, plunging, dipping, receding, burrowing, tunnelling, undermining, disembarking, landing
- **V** descend, fall, drop, tumble, sink, slump, settle, gravitate, submerge, dive, plunge, dip, recede; burrow, tunnel, undermine, alight, dismount, disembark, perch, land, settle, touch down, swoop

L2.4.3 Elevation
- **N** heightening, swelling, enlarging, enlargement, rise, raising, building, lifting, upraising, elevation, recovery; jacking up, propping up, hoisting/pulling up, boosting, boost; promotion,

    prolonging, intensifying, intensification, exaggeration, exaggerating, building up; lift, elevator, ladder, crane, hoist
A heightened, swollen, enlarged, risen, upraised, elevated, recovered; jacked-up, boosted; promoted, prolonged, intensified, exaggerated; hoisted
V heighten, swell, enlarge, raise, build, lift, upraise, elevate, recover, jack up, prop up, hoist/pull up, boost; promote, prolong, intensify, exaggerate, build up; hoist

L2.4.4 Depression
N depression, depressing, deflation, deflating, lowering, suppression, suppressing, belittling, cut-back, cut; dropping, drop, shedding, pouring; tripping, toppling, overthrow, overthrowing, flattening, knocking down, bowling over; pulling down, demolition, demolishing; undermining, collapsing, collapse, dilapidation, slump
A depressing, depressed, deflated, lowered, suppressed, belittling; dropped, shed, poured; tripped, toppled, overthrown, flattened, knocked down, bowled over; pulled down, demolished, undermined, collapsed, dilapidated; stooped, bent, leaning, cringing, cowering, bowed, kneeling, ducking, subdued, humbled, wilting, drooping
V depress, deflate, lower, suppress, belittle, cut back/down; let fall, drop, shed, pour; trip, topple, overthrow, flatten, knock down, bowl over; pull down, demolish, undermine, collapse, dilapidate, slump; stoop, bend, lean, cringe, cower, bow, kneel, duck, subdue, humble, wilt, droop

L2.4.5 Growing
N growth, sprout, sprouting, development, swelling, blowing up, inflation, fattening; increase, expansion, extension, enlargement, magnification, multiplication, amplification, proliferation; addition, supplement; adult, grown-up, maturity, maturation, ageing
A growing, sprouting, developing, swelling, inflated, fattened; increasing, expanding, expanded, extending, extended, enlarging, enlarged, magnifying, magnified, multiplying, amplifying, amplified, supplemented; adult, grown-up, mature, maturing, aged
V grow, sprout, develop, swell, blow up, inflate, fatten; increase, expand, extend, enlarge, magnify, multiply, amplify, double, proliferate; add to, supplement; grow up, mature, age

L2.4.6 Shrinking
N decrease, lessen, lessening, declining, sinking, shrinking, deflating, letting down, reduction, condensation; contraction, cut, diminishing, dwindling, falling off, melting
A decreasing, lessening, declining, sinking, shrinking, deflating, let down, reduced, condensed; contracted, cut, diminished, dwindling, fallen off, melted
V decrease, lessen, decline, sink, shrink, deflate, let down, reduce, condense; contract, cut, diminish, dwindle, fall off, melt

L2.4.7 Improvement
N improvement, advancement, progress, lengthening, broadening, deepening, heightening, strengthening, growing, growth, increase, gain, expansion, extension, flowering, blossoming, spreading, spread; acceleration, intensification, stimulation, reinforcement, relaxation, liberalisation
A improving, advancing, progressing, lengthening, broadening, deepening, heightening, strengthening; growing, increasing, gaining, expanding, flowering, blossoming, spreading; accelerating, intensifying, stimulating, reinforcing, reinforced, relaxing, relaxed, liberalising, liberalised
V improve, get better, better, advance, progress, lengthen, broaden, deepen, heighten, strengthen; grow, increase, gain, expand, extend, flower, blossom, spread; accelerate, intensify, stimulate, reinforce, relax, liberalise

L2.4.8 Deterioration
N deterioration, worsening, lessening, decreasing, weakening, diminishing, reducing, reduction, impairment; shrinking, abridging, abridgement, shortening, lightening, deflating, deflation, belittling, cheapening, dilating, dilation, subsiding, subsidence, coming down
A deteriorating, deteriorated, worsening, worse, lessening, decreasing, decreased, weakening, weakened, diminishing,

diminished, reducing, reduced; shrinking, shrunk, abridging, abridged, shortening, shortened, lightened, deflating, deflated, belittling, belittled, cheapened, dilating, dilated, subsiding, subsided
V deteriorate, get worse, worsen, lessen, decrease, weaken, diminish, reduce, impair, shrink, abridge, shorten, lessen, lighten, deflate, belittle, cheapen; dilute, subside, come down

L2.4.9 Liquid fall
N drop, drip, dribble, trickle, spill; running, stream, pouring, flow
A dropping, dropped, dribbling, dribbled, trickling, trickled, spilling, spilled
V drop, drip, dribble, trickle, spill; run, stream, pour, flow

L2.4.10 Temperature rise and fall
N heating, warming up, fever; cool, chill, freeze, shiver
A hot, heated, warm, warmed, feverish; cooled, chilled, frozen
V hot up, heat, heat up, warm, warm up, become feverish; cool, cool down, cool off, chill, freeze; shiver

L2.4.11 Rise and fall in value
N appreciation, gain, rise, inflation; depreciation, loss, fall, deflation
A appreciating, gaining, rising, inflated, inflationary; depreciating, losing, lost, falling, fallen, deflation, deflationary
V appreciate, gain, rise, inflate; depreciate, lose, fall, deflate

L2.4.12 Promotion and demotion
N promotion, upgrading; demotion, downgrading, reduction, relegation
A promoted, upgraded; demoted, downgraded, reduced, relegated
V promote, upgrade; demote, downgrade, reduce, relegate

L2.4.13 High and low spirits
A high-spirited, high, riding high, on a high, on cloud nine, living it up, head in the clouds, looking up, looking on the bright side; low-spirited, low, dispirited, fed up, down-hearted, downcast, down, pulling a long face, wearing a long face, having the cares of the world on one's shoulders
V brighten up, cheer up, perk up, buck up, look on the bright side, keep one's chin up, keep one's pecker up; pull a long face, wear a long face, have the cares of the world on one's shoulders, get one down, one's heart sinks

L2.5 Starting and stopping
L2.5.1 Beginning
N beginning, beginner, start, starter, commencement, introduction, dawn; launch, initiation, institution, innovation; starting up, establishment, starting out, setting out, origin, genesis, creation; birth, bud, shoot; appearance, entrance, emergence, taking off; opening, initial, starting point, zero hour, send-off; source, fount
A beginning, starting, commencing, introductory, dawning; initial, innovatory; establishing, established, original; budding; apparent, emergent; opening, initial
V begin, start, commence, resume, introduce, dawn; launch, initiate, institute, innovate; start up, establish, start out, set out; create, give birth, present; appear, enter, emerge, take off, open; switch on, set going, open up, break the ice, set the ball rolling; inaugurate, found, set up, establish

L2.5.2 Ending
N end, stop, halt, finish, shut-down, close, closure; cessation, expiry, death; petering out, fizzling out, drying up, running out, giving up, packing up; wearing out, breakdown; termination, conclusion, finality, finalisation; abortion; culmination, conclusion, completion, perfection, close, closure
A ended, stopped, halted, finished, shut-down, closed; expired, dead; fizzled out, dried up; worn out, broken down; terminal, concluding, conclusive, final; abortive, culmination, completing, perfect, closing
V end, stop, halt, finish, put an end to, shut up, shut down, close, close up, close down, cancel, cease, desist, refrain; expire, die, peter out, fizzle out; dry up, run out of, give up, pack up, wear off, wear out, break down; terminate, conclude, finalise, abort; culminate in, complete, perfect, close, finalise, relinquish

L2.6 Change

L2.6.1 Alteration
N alteration, change, modification, reform, reformation, reshaping, reorganisation, transformation, conversion, improvement, extension, amendment, correction, corrective, rectification, restoration, modernisation, up-date, up-dating, renewal, renovation, revival

A altered, changed, modified, reformed, reshaped, reorganised, transformed, converted, rectified, restored, modernised, renewed, renovated, revived

V alter, change, modify, remodel, reform, reshape, reorganise, transform, convert, improve, extend, tinker with, amend, correct, rectify, restore, modernise, up-date, renew, renovate, revive

L2.6.2 Replacement
N replacement, relief, substitution, substitute, stand-in, locum tenens, proxy, understudy, deputy, deputation, representative, representation, delegate, delegation, ambassador, embassy, envoy, agent

A replaced, replaceable, relief, deputy, representative, ambassadorial

V replace, relieve, substitute, stand in for, take somebody's place, understudy, deputise, represent, delegate

L2.7 Damage and repair

L2.7.1 General damage
N damage, cut, break, breakage, breach, bend, burst, injury, wear

A damaged, cut, broken, bent, burst, injured, worn

V damage, cut, break, bend, burst, injure, wear

L2.7.2 Impact
N impact, collision, bump, shock, crash, encounter, meeting, hammer, punch, mallet, knocker, knock, ram, bull-dozer, dent, rap, tap, pat, nudge; blow, stroke, hit, crack, cut; poke, punch, jab, hook; stamp, kick

A bumped, crashed, hammered, punched, knocked, rammed, bull-dozed, dented; rapped, tapped, patted, nudged, struck, cracked, dented, cutting, poking, punching, jabbing, hooking; stamped, kicked

V collide, make impact, touch, encounter, clash; ram, batter, dent; bull-doze; bump into, run over; strike, hit, slam, bang, knock; pat, flip, tickle, tap, clap, slap, smack, poke, punch, thump, beat up, pound, batter, knock out, stun; flatten, scratch, wound; strike, swipe, drive, cut crack, smash; kick, tread on, stamp on, ride over

L2.7.3 Disfigurement
N damage, impairment; spot, stain, mark, blemish, bruise; crack, fracture, chip, strain; scratch, scrape, graze, score; crumpling, creasing, crease, crushing, crush, squashing, squash; burning, burn, singeing, singe, scorching, scorch

A damaged, spoilt, marred, impaired; spotted, spotty, stained, marked, blemished, bruised; cracked, fractured, chipped, strained, scratched, scraped, grazed, scored; crumpled, creased, crushed, squashed; burnt, singed, scorched

V damage, spoil, mar, impair; spot, stain, mark, blemish, bruise; crack, fracture, chip, strain; scratch, scrape, graze, score; crumple, crease, crush, squash; burn, singe, scorch

L2.7.4 Loss of part
N breaking, breakage, break, snapping, snap, splitting, split, shearing; cut, severance, hack, slash, slice, chopping, chop; chiselling, carving, trimming, pruning, whittling; tearing, tear, ripping, rip, rending, rent, laceration, pulling apart

A broken, snapped, split, shorn, cut, severed, hacked, slashed, sliced, chopped; chiselled, carved, trimmed, pruned, whittled; torn, ripped, rent, lacerated

V break off, break away, snap, split, shear; cut, sever, hack, slash, slice, chop; chisel, carve, trim, prune, whittle; tear, rip, rend, lacerate, pull apart

L2.7.5 Disintegration
N smash, crash, shattering, splintering; shredding, grinding, mincing, grating; crumbling, powdering; bursting, burst, explosion, exploding

A smashed, crashed, shattered, splintered; shredded, ground, minced, grated; crumbled, powdered; burst, exploded, blown up, ruptured; distintegrated

V smash, crash, shatter, splinter; shred, grind, mince, grate; crumble, powder;

burst, explode, blow up, rupture; disintegrate, fall apart, come apart

L2.7.6 Distortion
N bending, bend, twisting, twist, buckling, buckle, dent, warping, disfigurement, distortion, mangling; stretching, swelling, shrinking, shrinkage, shrivelling; crushing, crush, squashing, squash, squeezing, squeeze, flattening
A bent, twisted, buckled, dented, warped, disfigured, distorted, mangled; stretched, swollen, shrunk, shrivelled; crushed, squashed, squeezed, flattened, flat
V bend, twist, buckle, dent, warp, disfigure, distort, mangle; stretch, swell, shrink, shrivel; crush, squash, squeeze, flatten

L2.7.7 Change of state
N decomposition, rotting, rot, rusting, rust, decaying, decay, mould; melting
A decomposed, rotten, rusty, decayed, mouldy; melted
V decompose, rot, rust, decay; melt

L2.7.8 Piercing
N piercing, pricking, prick, prickle, puncture, perforation, stabbing, stab, jabbing, jab, sticking; nicking, nick, slitting, slit, gashing, gash; biting, bite, stinging, sting
A pierced, pricked, punctured, perforated, stabbed, speared, stuck; nicked, slit, gashed; bitten, stung
V pierce, prick, puncture, perforate, stab, spear, jab, stick; nick, slit, gash; bite, sting

L2.7.9 Wear
N wearing away, wearing down, wearing out, wear, erosion, weathering; fraying; dilapidation
A worn, eroded, weathered; frayed; dilapidated
V wear away, wear down, wear out, erode, weather; fray, dilapidate

L2.7.10 Damage to the person
N cut, scratch, graze, bruise; burn, blister, scald, wound, injury, maiming, disfigurement, crippling, disablement, dismemberment, dismembering, mutilation, laming, blinding, deafening; ill-treatment, torture, poisoning
A cut, scratched, grazed, bruised; burnt, blistered, scalded; wounded, injured, maimed, disfigured, crippled, disabled, dismembered, mutilated, lamed, blind, deaf; tortured, poisoned
V cut, scratch, graze, bruise; burn, blister, scald; wound, injure, maim, disfigure, cripple, disable, dismember, mutilate, lame, blind, deafen; ill-treat, torture, poison

L2.7.11 Destruction
N destruction, wreckage, ruin, demolition; killing, murder, annihilation, wiping out; eradication, rooting out, stamping out, extermination, obliteration; devastation
A destroyed, wrecked, ruined, demolished; killed, dead, murdered, annihilated; exterminated, obliterated; devastated
V destroy, wreck, ruin, demolish; kill, murder, annihilate, wipe out; eradicate, root out, stamp our, exterminate, obliterate; devastate

L2.7.12 Repair
N repair, mending, amendment, restoration, renovation, renewal; fixing; darning, darn, patching, patch, stitching, stitch; reclamation, salvaging, salvage; adjustment, overhaul, putting right, rectification, correction, straightening; curing, healing, remedy, revival
A repaired, mended, restored, renovated, renewed; fixed; darned, patched, stitched; reclaimed, salvaged; adjusted, overhauled, rectified, corrected; straightened, cured, healed, remedied, remedial, revived
V repair, mend, amend, restore, renovate, renew; fix; darn, patch, stitch; reclaim, salvage; adjust, overhaul, put right, rectify, correct; straighten, cure, heal, make well, remedy, make better, revive

L2.8 *Integration and separation*

L2.8.1 Joining together
N joint, junction, connection, connector, attachment, affix, splice, splint; addition, bridge, span; tie, knot, yoke, harness, tether, link, chain; adhesive, glue, bond, bondage, fastening, fastener, cement
A joined, connected, attached, spliced; added, bridged, spanned; tied, knotted, yoked, harnessed, tethered, linked; stuck, glued, bonded, fastened, connected
V join, connect, attach, affix, spliced; add, bridge, span; tie, bind, knot, yoke, harness, tether, link, chain; stick, adhere, glue, bond, fasten, cement

L2.8.2 Integration
N unity, unison, integrity; junction,

consolidation, alliance, solidarity; fusion, welding; embodiment, marriage, harmony, harmonisation, interlocking; mixture, blend, combination, incorporation, affiliation, amalgamation, merger; relationship, connection, association, assimilation, interrelation; share, pool, cooperation, participation, participant
A united, unified, integral; amalgamated, merged, mingled; fused, welded; embodied, married, harmonised, interlocked; mixed, blended, combined, incorporated, affiliated
V unite, unify, integrate; coalesce, band together, consolidate, ally; fuse, weld; embody, marry, harmonise, interlock; mix, blend, combine, incorporate, affiliate, amalgamate, merge, mingle; relate, connect, associate, assimilate, interrelate; share, pool, cooperate, participate

L2.8.3   Collection
N collection, compilation, gathering, assembly, assemblage; concentration, congregation, meeting; group, herd, flock, shepherd; focus, accumulation; store class, classification; bundle, bunch, parcel, pack
A collected, compiled, gathered, assembled; concentrated, congregated; grouped, herded; focused, accumulated; stored, classed, classified; bundled, bunched, parcelled, packed
V collect, compile, gather, assemble, concentrate, congregate; meet, rejoin; group, herd, shepherd, focus, round up, accumulate; store, put together, class, classify; bundle, bunch, pack, parcel, piece together

L2.8.4   Separation
N separation, parting, isolation, disconnection, dislocation, removal, detachment; subtraction, division, dispersal, scattering, segregation; splitting, shredding, shred, chopping, cutting up, slicing, slice, mincing, mince, grinding, powdering, powder; dismantling, unloading; disintegration, break, fracture; escape, emergence
A separate, separated, parted, isolated, disconnected, dislocated, removed, detached; left, unstuck, unlocked, undone, peeled; subtracted, taken away, divided, broken up, split up, dispersed, scattered, segregated; split, shredded, diced, chopped, sliced, minced, ground, powdered; dismantled, unloaded; broken, fractured; escaped, freed
V separate, part, isolate, disconnect, dislocate, remove, detach; leave, unstick, unlock, undo, peel off; subtract, take away, divide, break up, split up, disperse, scatter, segregate; split, shred, dice, chop, cut up, slice, mince, grind, powder; dismantle, unload; disintegrate, fall apart, break, fracture; escape, get free, break out, emerge

L2.8.5   Removal of part
N removal, unfastening, untying; shredding, trimmings; peel, skin, shell, core, stone, bone
A removed, unfastened, untied; shed, trimmed, cast off; peeled, skinned, shelled, cored, stoned, boned, dressed
V remove, take away, unfasten, untie; shed, cut off, trim, cast off, peel, skin, shell, core, stone, bone; divest, get rid of, undress

L2.8.6   Help
N help, helper, helpfulness, aid, assistance, assistant, support, supporter, second, auxiliary, relief, benefit, benefactor, sponsorship, sponsor, grant, allowance, reward, maintenance, cooperation
A helpful, supportive, auxiliary, beneficial, rewarding, cooperative
V help, aid, assist, support, second, relieve, benefit, sponsor, grant, allow, reward, maintain, cooperate

L2.8.7   Cooperation
N cooperation, collaboration, collaborator, team work; plot, conspiracy, conspirator, participation, participant, mutual assistance, assistant; association, associate, partnership, partner, federation, corporation; colleague, fellow, comrade, accomplice, workmake
A cooperative, collaborative, conspiratorial, mutual, federal, corporative
V cooperate, collaborate; plot, conspire; participate, assist, associate with, partner, federate

L2.8.8   Rubbish
N rubbish, trash, waste, scrap, junk, jumble, garbage, refuse, lumber, litter, sewage; nonsense, twaddle, rot

A unwanted, trashy, wasted, scrapped, disposable
V throw away, scrap, discard, get rid of, dismantle, cast, jettison, dispose of, squander

L2.8.9 Waste collection and salvage
N dump, tip, scrap-heap, scrap-yard; rubbish bin, dust bin, waste-paper basket; sewer, drain, sump, gutter, ditch; wastage, leakage, outflow, exhaust; scavenger, recycling, rescue, recovery, reclamation, re-use, salvage
A dumped, scrapped, ditched; obsolete; redundant, unwanted, useless, worthless, reject; recycled, rescued, recovered, reclaimed, re-used, salvaged
V dump, tip, scrap, throw away, reject; scavenge, recycle, rescue, recover, reclaim, re-use, salvage

L2.8.10 Remains
N remains, remainder, residue; sediment, sludge; rubble, debris, wreck, wreckage; dregs, leavings, droppings, pickings, scrap, crumb, remnant, odds and ends, cast-offs, left-overs; dead wood, castaway, outcast
A remaining, residual; sedimentary; wrecked; scrapped; polluted, contaminated; cast-off
V remain; wreck; scrap; reject, leave; pollute, contaminate, cast off